1,000,000 Books
are available to read at

Forgotten Books

www.ForgottenBooks.com

Read online
Download PDF
Purchase in print

ISBN 978-1-330-72691-4
PIBN 10097596

This book is a reproduction of an important historical work. Forgotten Books uses state-of-the-art technology to digitally reconstruct the work, preserving the original format whilst repairing imperfections present in the aged copy. In rare cases, an imperfection in the original, such as a blemish or missing page, may be replicated in our edition. We do, however, repair the vast majority of imperfections successfully; any imperfections that remain are intentionally left to preserve the state of such historical works.

Forgotten Books is a registered trademark of FB &c Ltd.
Copyright © 2018 FB &c Ltd.
FB &c Ltd, Dalton House, 60 Windsor Avenue, London, SW19 2RR.
Company number 08720141. Registered in England and Wales.

For support please visit www.forgottenbooks.com

1 MONTH OF FREE READING

at

www.ForgottenBooks.com

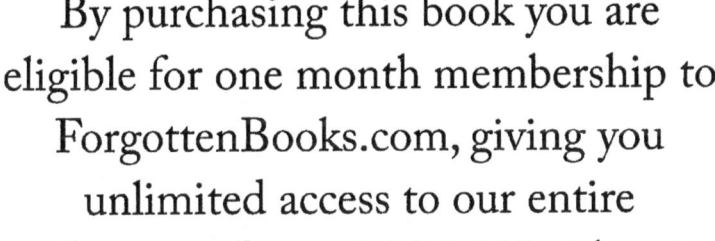

By purchasing this book you are eligible for one month membership to ForgottenBooks.com, giving you unlimited access to our entire collection of over 1,000,000 titles via our web site and mobile apps.

To claim your free month visit:
www.forgottenbooks.com/free97596

* Offer is valid for 45 days from date of purchase. Terms and conditions apply.

English
Français
Deutsche
Italiano
Español
Português

www.forgottenbooks.com

Mythology Photography **Fiction** Fishing Christianity **Art** Cooking Essays Buddhism Freemasonry Medicine **Biology** Music **Ancient Egypt** Evolution Carpentry Physics Dance Geology **Mathematics** Fitness Shakespeare **Folklore** Yoga Marketing **Confidence** Immortality Biographies Poetry **Psychology** Witchcraft Electronics Chemistry History **Law** Accounting **Philosophy** Anthropology Alchemy Drama Quantum Mechanics Atheism Sexual Health **Ancient History** **Entrepreneurship** Languages Sport Paleontology Needlework Islam **Metaphysics** Investment Archaeology Parenting Statistics Criminology **Motivational**

THE HISTORY OF
THE LITHUANIAN NATION

The History of The Lithuanian Nation

AND

Its Present National Aspirations

By

Kunigas Antanas Jusaitis

Master of Laws of the University of Fribourg, Switzerland

Translated from the Lithuanian

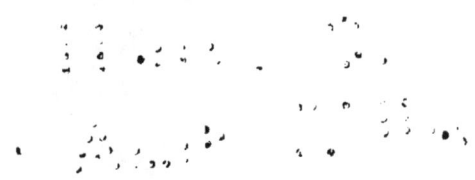

Published by
The Lithuanian Catholic Truth Society
1918

Copyright, 1918, by
LITHUANIAN CATHOLIC TRUTH SOCIETY.

Translated from Lithuanian as published in a weekly magazine, Zvaigzde, in 1917, by A. Milukas & Company, Philadelphia, Pa.

PROEM

Out of the depths there comes a cry from a nation which for centuries has been forced to be inarticulate. It is not a demand for privilege, for territory to which it might have only a historical claim; it is a cry for life, and if we really believe in our own professions, if the traditions of 1776 have not been effaced, if the definition of self-determinism with which President Wilson is changing the evil systems of lust and avarice in Europe and the rest of the world—we Americans must listen to this cry from the core of the hearts of the Lithuanians. We cannot close our ears to it.

We know the story of Poland—when a King's mistress stifled the protests of France, and even the cynical Frederick of Prussia wondered how the Empress Maria Teresa could square her conscience to her confessor; we know the story of Ireland, of the terrible wrongs which liberal-minded Englishmen regret as deeply as the Irishmen themselves, we are beginning to understand by what horrible oppression in Schleswig-Holstein the German Empire made itself dominant, and developed that system of autocracy toward which at times every European nation has had tendencies; but the story of the Lithuanians—blood-brothers with us in their love of freedom—is new to most of us.

PROEM

To me, dwelling in the centre of diplomatic "conversations" for many years, it is an old and appalling story. No man can know a Lithuanian without discovering that a never-dying passion for the independence of his country is eating into his soul. And Why? This book tells us, with a simplicity and power which no man who believes in a national, as well as an individual conscience, ought to resist. This volume is short; it contains no idle words, no mere rhetoric; it tells the story of a wronged nation so convincingly that any analysis of its contents in this little Preface would be utterly superfluous. There is no statement in it that is not true.

I, whom three Presidents of the United States—Mr. Roosevelt and Mr. Taft and President Wilson, have trusted to represent the American people in a little nation, that of Denmark, because both by inheritance and conviction I believed that democracy could only be true to its principles when it so applied them that these little nations might be free to develop their own culture—have a right to speak for Lithuania as a nation, and to voice the belief that, in the great reckoning which the world awaits to-day, the demand of this most oppressed of little countries shall receive the tenderest sympathy and the most practical support from her just and generous brethren, the American people.

MAURICE FRANCIS EGAN.

CONTENTS

CHAPTER I

The Nations of the Lithuanian (Aistian) Race; Their Territory, Origin, Language, Religion, Character, Culture Before the Beginning of Their History (Before 1200 A. D.) 1

CHAPTER II

The History of the Lithuanian Nation and State to the Death of Vitautas 11

CHAPTER III

The Relations with the Poles which Began Under Grand Duke Jagela; the Rulers of the same Lithuanian Dynasty for both States; the Long-Continued Personal Union of both States Repeatedly Renewed; Alliances with Poland Contracted many Times; Weakening of the Supreme Power of Government in Lithuania by the Introduction of Polish States Laws; the Spread of Polonization in Lithuania and with It the Demoralization of the National Consciousness of the Lithuanian People. The Consequences of these Relations is the Polish-Lithuanian Union at Lublin 23

CONTENTS

CHAPTER IV

The Juristic Appraisement of the Bonds Between Lithuanian and Polish States which Existed Before and After the Union of Lublin 38

CHAPTER V

The Causes of the Downfall of the Polish (and with It the Lithuanian) State; the Union with Lithuania Is the True Reason for the Growth of the Polish Nation and State, but, at the same Time, the Cause of Internal Anarchy and the Downfall of that State 52

CHAPTER VI

The Survival of the National Consciousness of the Lithuanians up to the Present Day Through the Preservation of Their Own Language, Traditions, and the Expression of that Consciousness in Their Literature; the Rise and Expansion among the Lithuanians of the Idea of National Independence from Dangerous Foreign Influence; the Present Cultural and Economic Growth of the Nation 63

CHAPTER VII

The Present National Aspirations of the Lithuanians: the Political Unity and Independence of All Parts of the Lithuanian Nation now Under Different Governments (Russian and German); Freedom from Foreign Influences; the Preservation of One and Sole Lithuanian Language as the National Tongue; Relations with the Poles, White Russians, and Letts 81

CONTENTS

CHAPTER VIII

Is Lithuania, as a State, Possible? Ability of Lithuanians for Statesmanship; the Right to Independence of Nations which Have Lost or Have Never Had Their Own Government; the Fate of Small Nations in Foreign States (viz., Russia); Have the Lithuanians a Sufficient Number of Educated Men to Conduct the Government of State? Area and Population of Lithuania Compared with the Different Independent European States 91

Appendix 109

CHAPTER I

THE NATIONS OF THE LITHUANIAN (AISTIAN) RACE; THEIR TERRITORY, ORIGIN, LANGUAGE, RELIGION, CHARACTER, CULTURE BEFORE THE BEGINNING OF THEIR HISTORY (BEFORE 1200 A. D.)

THE Lithuanians are among the smaller nations of Europe. In the latter part of the nineteenth century this nation was so humiliated by the Polonization of its higher classes and by suppression of its nationality by the Russian Government that even its name has been denied a place among the nations of the world. Yet there was a time, in the fourteenth and fifteenth centuries, when Lithuania was one of the largest empires in Europe.

In speaking of Lithuania one must consider it in these three aspects: First, the mighty Lithuanian state of the fifteenth century, the historical Lithuania, which extended from the Baltic Sea at Polangen and the mouth of the Niemen River to the Black Sea between the Dnieper and Dniester rivers, where now is situated the city of Odessa, and from the Bug River in the west to the river Oka in the east. Second, Lithuania taken as a territory populated with descendants of the Lithuanian race, where now a part of them use the White Russian language and a few, who live in scattered groups, use the Polish, but where in the earlier centuries the people were of the same Lithuanian blood, the same Lithuanian language, and of the same Lithuanian religion and customs peculiar to themselves—such is Lithuania in a wide ethnographical sense. It embraces the former Russian governments of Kovno, Vilna, Suvalki, and Grodno, and East Prussia to the River Alle and the city of Labiau on the Baltic coast.

But in a strict ethnographical sense, and this is the third aspect of the case, Lithuania is a country where the population even now speaks the Lithuanian language, has not forgotten its glorious historical past, and is animated by the same national ideal—the political unity of the entire Lithuanian territory under one national government, their own state authority.

That land which is even now Lithuanian in its language and is the kernel of historic Lithuania comprises the entire government of Kovno, Vilna (except two counties in the east, Disna and Vileika), a part of Grodno north of the Niemen, Suvalki (except the county of Augustovo), parts of the government of Courland, and the northeastern part of Eastern Prussia extending to the Pregel River.

The Lithuanians, together with their kinsmen, the Letts, who live in the governments of Courland, Livonia, and Vitebsk, and the old Prussians* (Borussi), who occupied the territory to the west of the Lithuanians up to the river Vistula, but a part of whom were annihilated by the Teutons in the wars in the thirteenth century and the remnants of whom were definitely Germanized about the end of the

---

* The Prussians mentioned here are not to be identified with the Prussians of modern times. Whenever the term Prussians is used in this book it refers to the Borussians or Prussians from whom the name of the modern Prussians is derived but with whom they have no racial connection. The name came to the present Prussians by conquest. The Encyclopædia Britannica in its article on the Lithuanians gives the Borussians or Prussians as one of the three main branches of the Lithuanian stem in the tenth century; but it states: "The Lithuanian territory thus lay open to foreign invasions, and the Russians as well as the German crusaders availed themselves of the opportunity. The Borussians soon fell under the dominion of Germans, and ceased to constitute a separate nationality, leaving only their name to the state which later became Prussia."

seventeenth century, all belong to the Indo-European nations. The Lithuanians are not of the Slavonic race, nor are they of the German race, with which they have as little in common as they have with the Latins, Persians, or Greeks. Their Lithuanian language with its old forms is so important to the science of linguistic study that it is placed in a class with the Sanscrit. They are the aboriginal inhabitants of their land; no other race inhabited it before them. Anthropological researches show that the human skulls unearthed in the graveyards of Lithuania belong to people of the same anthropological class as the present Lithuanians. The latest theory in history about the first Indo-European settlements, supported by archæology, anthropology, and linguistic researches, places these settlements in the middle of Europe and in the south Russian steppes; it rejects the first accepted supposition about the coming of Indo-Europeans from Asia; they had emigrated to Asia from Europe. The suppositions of some Lithuanian writers that Lithuanians had come from Asia Minor are not sound.

Before their adoption of Christianity the

Lithuanians, together with their kinsmen, the Letts and the Prussians,* had their own religion, with an established hierarchy, in which were different ranks of divines ruled over by a single high priest. The supreme god was Perkunas, god of the heavens and of thunder. He corresponds to the Roman Jupiter or the Greek Zeus. There were other gods who were the personification of nature and of places—of homes, rivers, forests; and guardian deities of the people's industries, such as farming and hunting; and gods of love and of war.

Lately a foreigner who visited Lithuania, which is now occupied by German armies,† wrote of the character of Lithuanians:

"They are a quiet, polite people, peacefully following their occupations of farming and other work about their homes, and seeing them no one could even think that this was the same nation that in the thirteenth and fourteenth centuries showed itself so valiant, that it created such a great kingdom and conquered such an extent of land."

* Not to be identified with the modern Prussians (see footnote, p. 3).
† This article was written in 1917 when the German armies were still occupying Lithuania.

In the beginning of the thirteenth century the Lithuanians united in one state so as to defend themselves from attack by the Slavs and Germans, and began a fierce war with their aggressors to save a place for themselves in the world. During the thirteenth century the Slav and German writers called the Lithuanians "the pagan-Lithuanians, wildmen, cruel, plunderers, living as animals." Relying on this statement a great many Poles of our day remind the Lithuanians that they should be grateful to them, because they, the Poles, uniting with the Lithuanians, made them a civilized people.

To this we may reply that these writings are not the unbiassed opinions of neighbors but the calumnies of enemies, who, attacking and murdering the Lithuanians, received from them the same treatment. We have reports concerning the character of Lithuanians and their civilization of those days from other more unbiassed sources.

Duesburg writes (Script. rer. prus. I, 52) that Zambia and particularly Sudavia were wealthy and thickly populated (opulenta et populosa). Sudavians occupied the southern part of the government of Suvalki and a part of Prussia farther to the west. Adam of Bremen (De situ Daniæ, cap. 227), in the eleventh century, and Helmhold (Chron. slavor., I, cap. 1) in the twelfth century, writing about the same Lithuanians and Prussians,* call them "homines humanissimi" and only regret that, although they are so good, they are not Christians. Jornandes, Bishop of the Goths, who wrote about the year 550 A. D., calls the Aistians "pacatum hominum genus omnino" (De rebus Geticis, V, 25). Tacitus (Germania, cap. 45) calls the Aistians (those same Lithuanians and Prussians) peaceful and more industrious than the Germans, and testifies that they employ themselves in growing grain and vegetables (frumenta ceterosque fructus), and also navigate the seas.

The archæology of the present day gives us an idea of the culture of the old Lithuanian nations. It is known that in the Neolithic times (between 3000 and 1500 B. C.) all kinds of grain—barley, rye, and oats—were grown in Lithuania (Sitzungsberichte d. Altertumsgesell-

* Not to be identified with the modern Prussians (see footnote, p. 3).

schaft, "Prussia," 1909, Heft 22, p. 502). In the ruins of Mikenai, in Greece (about 1500 B. C.), a quantity of beads made of Baltic amber were found. Most of the amber is found on the Baltic coast, where was the home of the old Prussians and Lithuanians; a clear proof of the commerce of the Lithuanians with these far-off lands, the lands of early culture, if not directly, then through intervening nations. S. Mueller, Schumann, Oskar Montelius showed that in the Hallstatt's period, in the first days of iron in Europe (1000 to 400 B. C.) not only was grain grown in Lithuania but domestic animals were kept, and linen as well as woollen clothing was worn. In the cemeteries of middle Europe of the Hallstatt's period likewise were found ornaments made of amber.

The archæologists, Tischler, Lissauer, Bezzenberger, and others show that, judging by excavations of the cemeteries of Lithuania and Prussia, beginning with the times of Christ and up to the invasion of Prussia by the Teutonic Crusaders, the wealth and culture of the Lithuanians stood very high. The Lithuanians had weapons, farming and industrial implements, and all kinds of expensive ornaments. The number and variety of articles found in the burial-grounds are astonishing ("unser Staunen erregen"—Tischler): iron knives, chisels, sickles, spears, swords, bronze bridles, spurs, bracelets, buckles, clasps, glass beads, and a number of gold and silver ornaments. Especially well-made things of bronze and other metals show a highly perfected technic in metal-working (Heydeck). Tischler writes that excavations in the cemeteries of the period when Prussian paganism was coming to its end—about the time when the Crusaders made their appearance—furnish evidences of a magnificent Lithuanian culture (Ueber die Gliederung der Urgesch. Ostpreusens, p. 7); and Heydeck asserts that the Lithuanian and Prussian culture of those days was in no way lower than that of Teutonic Crusaders.

If according to testimony quoted Lithuanians in the sixth and also in the eleventh centuries were "pacatum hominum genus omnino," "homines humanissimi," then they were not robbers, nor wildmen, nor were they living as animals. If before the coming of Teutonic Crusaders to Prussia Lithuanian culture was not inferior to that of Crusaders, then the Lithuanian culture of twelfth and thirteenth centuries could not have been low. But the continuous wars, during centuries, with Slavs (Russians and Poles) and with Germans, and then with Tartars, greatly weakened the Lithuanians, diminished their numbers, destroyed their material welfare, and lowered their culture.

CHAPTER II

THE HISTORY OF THE LITHUANIAN NATION AND STATE TO THE DEATH OF VITAUTAS

THE Lithuanians, according to archæology, have lived in the region they now occupy for several thousand years. The ancient writers called the Lithuanian nation "Aistians." We find in Ptolemy's writings (III, 5) in the second century A. D. the mention of Galindæ (Prussians) and Sudeni (Lithuanians) as the names of two Aistian tribes—names later used among Lithuanians.

The Lithuanians did not take part in the migrations of the nations, except perhaps one or another of the smaller tribes on the outskirts of the inhabited territories of Lithuania which may have joined the emigration of the larger Teutonic tribes. The cause of this was the state of the culture of the Lithuanians at that period. The main occupation of all the Lithuanian nation was agriculture, which always requires fixed settlements; and the wealth of the nation, stored up in peace through many centuries of hard labor, could not be taken with them from one place to another after the manner of barbarous nomadic tribes. On this account, as we see in history, the civilized and settled nations often are conquered by others less civilized, but never change their settlements in order to move away from the conquerors or to conquer another country. For instance, the civilization of Sumerians on the plains of Mesopotamia in ante-Babylonian times was conquered several times by the nomadic hordes from Arabia, until finally these people had mixed with their conquerors and accepted their Semitic language; the civilization of Greece and Rome was destroyed hy the barbaric Teutons (Germans); the little kingdoms of Chanaan were conquered by the nomadic Hebrews; and the great civilized Chinese Empire was conquered by the Mongolians.

During the first centuries of the Christian era the Lithuanian nations had intimate dealings with the German Goths. This is shown by the various words, with a Gothic stem, which are found in the Prussian and Lithuanian languages. Until the tenth century the Lithuanian nations lived without larger political organization. The one thing in common was the same faith, similar language, and the same customs. But during the tenth century the Slavs began to harass the peaceful Lithuanians from the south and east and this forced them to form military organizations under the leadership of their Dukes-Kunigas. At the beginning of the thirteenth century we see from chronicles that in Lithuania proper, not including Prussia, there were about twenty powerful Dukes.

Duke Mindaugas (Mindove) was the first to organize the greater part of the Lithuanian territories in one state. He was the first author of the Lithuanian state and the first organizer of the Lithuanian nation.

Mindaugas did not succeed, however, in uniting all the nation. There remained Jacvingi in the south and Samogitians in the west who were not under his domain. He pushed the boundary in the east beyond Smolensk. His work of organizing was delayed by the unceasing attacks of the German hordes and the wars with the Galician Dukes, which caused his untimely death. He was baptized a Catholic; received the King's crown from Pope Innocent IV, becoming the King of Lithuania in the year 1253 A. D. He died in 1263, treacherously assassinated during a campaign, just when he had arranged everything for the liberation of Samogithians from the oppression of the Teutonic Order of Crusaders and for uniting them under his rule.

After the death of Mindaugas a quarrel arose among the local Dukes in Lithuania, but the idea of a Grand Duke proved to be ineradicable. Chaos did not cease until the beginning of the fourteenth century. From 1315 to 1340 Gediminas ruled as the Grand Duke. Lithuania had become so strong a nation during his reign that all the neighboring states had to acknowledge Gediminas. He united the entire nation except the Lithuanians at the mouth of the Niemen and by the river Pregel, who were for a long time under the rule of the German Knights. Through him Lithuania reached her natural boundaries in the south and east to the rivers Pripet and Dnieper.

The aim of the heirs of Gediminas should have been to collect all of Lithuania's strength, to overpower both Teutonic knightly Orders, to free the Lithuanian neighbors, Letts and Prussians, to unite all into one state. The nation as it was left by Gediminas was sufficiently powerful to accomplish these aims. The Prussians and the Letts from the very time of their subjection to the German Knights revolted more than once against them. Shortly after Gediminas's death all the Letts revolted against the Germans. It was the most suc cessful revolt; with a few exceptions all the towns were taken by the Letts. By the destruction of the Livonian Order and the freeing of the Letts the expulsion of the German Order from Prussia would have been assured. But the Lithuanians did not lend a hand to their kinsmen, the Letts; the German Knights from Prussia came to assist their brother Knights in Riga, and they both suppressed the revolt.

The successor of Gediminas, Algirdas, made a capital error by not envisaging his true objective. Instead of occupying for Lithuania the seashore from the Vistula to the Narva and uniting the Prussians and Letts to Lithuania, and thus strengthening the foundation of the state by nations of the same race and similar language, he deputed his brother, the knightly Kestutis, to protect Lithuania with the Samogitians from the robber Orders, while he himself turned all the remaining strength of the state to the east against the Slavs and Tartars. True, by his victories he made Lithuania a great empire, which covered almost half of modern Russia, extending from the Baltic to the Black Seas, but by doing this he renounced nearly half the nations of the Lithuanian race and part of it, the Prussians, he left to perdition. On the other hand, he brought into the state a greater proportion of foreigners than of his own people and placed the Lithuanian nation in peril of becoming a non-Lithuanian state.

The son of Algirdas and his successor, Jagela (Jagello), committed a great political error, if we may so mildly define his dealings with the Lithuanian state. The neighbors, the Poles, of that time were ruled by a Queen, a young maiden, Hedwig. The Poles under the reign of Louis the Hungarian had gained such experience by electing the ruler of another nation their King as to know that if he continues to live in his former state their nation is at best as one without a King, and uprisings result. I say at best, for the result may be more serious: for instance, the territory may fall under the influence of another nation and may lose its independence.

The Polish magnates gave their Princess Hedwig's hand in marriage to Jagela (Jagello) on condition that he be King of the Poles. The duty of the King of the Poles was to be King of the Poles only, that is, to live in Cracow, Poland, and to unite Lithuania to Poland; to be definite, this meant that Lithuania would be annexed to Poland as a Polish province. This appeared to Jagela a small price, for as King of Poland he would also govern the provinces. To introduce the Catholic faith into Lithuania was demanded by ordinary political wisdom, for Poland being a Catholic nation would be stronger if all her provinces should have one and the same faith. That it was not an idealistic task to destroy paganism in Lithuania we gather from this, that various later privileges, for instance, the citizenship of Lithuania, were granted to Catholics only and the Lithuanians of the Eastern rite (orthodox) were not granted this privilege and were forbidden even to enter into matrimonial relationship with Catholics. Jagela agreed, and for the kingdom of Poland he gave the Poles his native country, Lithuania, founded by the works of the great leaders, Algirdas and Gediminas, his father and grandfather, and by the blood of Lithuanians. Having been crowned King of the Poles, but not of the Lithuanians, and having settled in Poland, Jagela appointed a Viceroy to rule Lithuania, and even stationed a Polish garrison in Vilna. To call the ruler of a nation a traitor is not befitting, and as it did not seem possible to the Lithuanians of those times, but that they thus understood the act of Jagela we see from the fact that they arose against the King's Viceroy, wishing to give the throne of Lithuania to Vitautas, their leader, and by this to show that they acknowledged Jagela as having been deprived of the Grand Duke's office. Jagela was forced to recognize Vitautas as the Grand Duke of Lithuania; with Poland there was left only an agreement of mutual assistance in case of war. The reign of Vitautas (1392–1430) constitutes the period of the greatest manifestation of Lithuanian power abroad. He combined into one powerful state the whole empire of

Algirdas and all the Lithuanian dukedoms; the authority of Grand Duke he made autocratic, even toward the magnates. In the very beginning of his reign opposition was made by the more influential Dukes; but the more dangerous of these he dispossessed, and those remaining were forced blindly to obey his orders. Having strengthened his power at home he wanted to unite the Russians and their lords, the Tartars, to Lithuania; but he was utterly defeated by the Tartars at Vorskla in 1399. Hedwig, wife of Jagela, died in that year. The Poles, receiving no benefit from Jagela, their King through marriage to Hedwig, could have removed him from the rulership of Poland; but this would have caused Vitautas uneasiness, for Jagela might then have become a pretender to the Lithuanian throne, and so, to assist him, Vitautas, in 1401, made a treaty by which he acknowledged Jagela his successor to the throne of Lithuania.

Shortly after the Vorskla defeat Vitautas succeeded in strengthening his power, and by his diplomacy he so managed that the Tartars were kept as his vassals during his reign; he kept their Khans under his protection and they accorded him their military support. Now he set his face against the deadly enemies of Lithuania in the west, the Teutonic Knights of the Cross. Within a few years he collected his forces for the decisive war. It was difficult for him to induce the Poles to wage war, but the Knights of the Cross themselves helped him in that respect by attacking the Poles. Finally Jagela declared war. Vitautas drew not only the Lithuanians into this war but the Russians, the Tartars, and hired the army of the Czechs from western Europe. He even helped the Poles by sending them necessary provisions for the war. The battle was fought at Gruenwald and Tanenberg in Prussia (1410). Vitautas arranged the armies for battle. He was the most active leader in the battle, and by his strategy victory was won. The power of the Teutonic Order was crushed.

If this victory had been made the most of, the Order of the Knights of the Cross would have been completely destroyed. But the Poles occupying the Prussian cities immediately united with Poland, and by their greediness forced Vitautas to opposite action. Vitautas himself saved the Order from utter ruin by not assisting the Poles to wage war, and while taking part in the treaty of Thorn he arranged the easiest terms possible for the Order. He had to contend with the Poles in the future, who continuously exhibited pretensions toward the state of Lithuania. He did not wish the Poles to grow considerably in strength. The Order was necessary to him in his relations with the Poles.

On October 2, 1413, an important union was made in Horodlo between the Lithuanians and the Poles by which both parties remained equal; both promised at the death of either ruler to elect a new one in his place. At the death of a Polish King his successor was to be elected by the Polish magnates together with the magnates of Lithuania and their Grand Duke; and, vice versa, the Grand Duke of Lithuania was to be elected by the Lithuanian magnates together with the magnates of Poland and their King. Here the rights of both were equal. Lithuania was second by title only; Poland was a kingdom, Lithuania a grand duchy. In a protocol, Lithuania as a duchy was joined to Poland, a kingdom. Lithuania's title was lower, although that duchy was thrice larger than the Polish Kingdom and much more powerful. But in the opinion of those times the title meant much. This joining of their country to a foreign country the Lithuanians, as their attitude in the near future showed, did not consider seriously.

At the end of his reign, having no son as an heir who should insure Lithuania's independence, making her in all things equal to Poland, Vitautas decided to crown himself as King of Lithuania; but the act of coronation did not occur, as robbers sent by the Polish politicians opposing Vitautas took away the crown, which was being carried to Vitautas by the emissaries of the Emperor Sigismund, and Vitautas died suddenly during the festivities of his coronation.

CHAPTER III

THE RELATIONS WITH THE POLES WHICH BEGAN UNDER GRAND DUKE JAGELA; THE RULERS OF THE SAME LITHUANIAN DYNASTY FOR BOTH STATES; THE LONG-CONTINUED PERSONAL UNION OF BOTH STATES REPEATEDLY RENEWED; ALLIANCES WITH POLAND CONTRACTED MANY TIMES; WEAKENING OF THE SUPREME POWER OF GOVERNMENT IN LITHUANIA BY THE INTRODUCTION OF POLISH STATES LAWS; THE SPREAD OF POLONIZATION IN LITHUANIA AND WITH IT THE DEMORALIZATION OF THE NATIONAL CONSCIOUSNESS OF THE LITHUANIAN PEOPLE. THE CONSEQUENCES OF THESE RELATIONS IS THE POLISH-LITHUANIAN UNION AT LUBLIN

THE Lithuanian magnates did not desire the union that was made by Jagela and Vitautas at the instigation of Poles, and at the first opportunity they showed that they did not acknowledge it.

After the death of Vitautas the Lithuanians, disregarding the Horodlo union, elected as their Grand Duke, in 1430, Svitrigaila without the Polish participation and against their wishes. Svitrigaila did not acknowledge the union during all his reign, and even made King Jagela a prisoner because the Poles took some cities of Podolia. He released Jagela only after his promise to restore those cities to Lithuania.

His rival for power, Sigismund, son of Kestutis, in order to obtain the Polish aid in the war with Svitrigaila, renewed the union in 1432; but this union was broken by the Lithuanians after the death of Sigismund, son of Kestutis, when they elected as their Grand Duke, Casimir, son of Jagela. And so it went on: the union was continually being patched up by the Poles and always, at the first opportunity, it was broken by the Lithuanians. Sometimes during the reign of the same ruler these unions were made several times, and there were innumerable quarrels between Lithuanians and Poles at the special conventions called expressly for the formation of these unions. That was so until the last union at Lublin in 1569.

The Poles wanted a complete union of Lithuania and Poland by the conversion of Lithuania into a Polish province. This they expressed openly at the convention at Lublin in 1448; they proposed to make of both states one Polish Kingdom; to make of Lithuania a Polish province, the Lithuanians to become Polish subjects on the same footing as true Poles; all the gentry to enjoy the same privileges. The Lithuanians, on the contrary, did not wish to renounce the independence of their state; they only agreed to an alliance with Poland and to the defensive bond against their foes.

But the continual proposals by the Poles of union, the personal union with Poland of a hundred years, except for two intervals, the weakening of the government in Lithuania by the privileges of the gentry, the long-established relations of Lithuanian and the Polish gentry, accomplished its purpose: the Polish designs upon the independent prerogatives of Lithuania as a separate state were partly successful.

* * *

The Polish magnates were very anxious to gain possession of lands in Lithuania, but the laws of Lithuania denied ownership to foreigners. Importunate demands by Poles that Lithuanians give them Volinia and Podolia, their nearest and most fertile lands, resulted; and when the Lithuanians refused so to diminish their state, the Poles demanded the abolition of the boundary between Poland and Lithuania. Here lies the true significance of the continual Polish demands to unite Lithuania to Poland. We find that having obtained at the Lublin union the most fertile lands of Lithuania, all territory south of the Pripet River, the Poles no longer approach the Lithuanians with projects for new unions.

After the death of King Vladislaus III in 1444, the Poles invited the Grand Duke of Lithuania, Casimir, son of Jagela, to be their King. Only after three years did the Lithuanians grant him permission to go to Poland; and for forty-five years, till his death in 1492, they remained without their ruler. In this policy the Polish politicians must have seen the easiest way to extinguish the separate rule in Lithuania; for, as they proclaimed as their King every Grand Duke elected by the Lithuanians, they deprived Lithuania of a ruler. Polish privileges were constituted a bait with which the Poles caught Lithuanian noblemen, and kept them attached to themselves; a most successful policy to render Lithuania powerless, and thus to sweep aside all her opposition, although used perhaps unwittingly by the Poles only to weaken the supreme authority of the state.

The first privileges were accorded to Lithuanian noblemen by Jagela in 1387. In the union of 1413 those privileges were confirmed: the ownership of large estates; the release from all active duties toward the Grand Duke, excepting war service, and that of restoring the fortified cities; the right to take part in the council of the Grand Duke, and to choose a ruler—the occupation of the throne was now to be determined by election. These rights served as a constitution for the country. At first they were given to the Catholics, although under Sigismund, son of Kestutis, they were extended among the Orthodox; but later the Orthodox were always isolated and wronged. This separation between Catholics and Orthodox had sown antagonism in Lithuania between the Catholic and the Orthodox citizens; and from this had arisen in a short time a civil war between Svitrigaila and the adherents of Sigismund—in truth, between the parties of the Catholics and Russians. Later it served the Russians as a pretext to cling to Moscow.

Every later Grand Duke or King distributed new privileges in order to keep himself on both thrones—for example, by the renunciation of fees, the state collected for the peasants belonging to noblemen; by the gift to the landowners of the right to administer justice to their peasants and to exact the pecuniary penalties; by forbidding peasants to possess land, and so benefiting of noblemen; by the interdiction of children of bond-slaves from attending schools and learning trades.

These privileges were diminishing the Grand Duke's power and wealth by making noblemen the absolute lords over their subject peasants. About 1550 slavery in Lithuania and Russia had already reached its highest degree: in some places the peasants had to work for their masters six days a week, and they belonged entirely to them. The nobleman did with the peasant slave as he wished, and took from him what he wished. Within twenty-six years after the union of Lublin, there arose in the Russian Provinces of Lithuania a formidable insurrection of slaves against noblemen, the insurrection of Nalivaika in 1595.

These privileges made peasants always more dependent on the noblemen, and the noblemen always less dependent on the supreme government of the state. After the distribution of the Grand Duke's wealth and income, the treasury of Lithuania was empty. Before the Lublin union, the Lithuanian minister of finances, Paul Naruszevicz, complained to the King that the Lithuanian treasury needed immediate help as means were lacking to keep the fortresses on the boundary-line and their garrisons. There was no income in the treasury; he himself had even pawned his estates and loaned money wherever possible. There were no means to keep up the army; to defend the borders of the state; to punish wrong-doers. The state organization and discipline created by the works of Gediminas, Algirdas, and Vitautas was destroyed by the Polish unions and the privileges; anarchy was spreading. This disorganization was encouraged by the fact that Lithuania actually was without a ruler. The Grand Duke resided in Poland, and was interested in Lithuania's affairs only so far as to distribute to his Polish favorites the estates in Lithuania—the Lithuanian offices or towns.

During this time the Poles were trying by various means to force themselves into Lithuania. Polonism was spreading more and more among Lithuanians, and began to undermine Lithuanian nationalism.

At the convention in Brest, in 1542 and 1544, the Lithuanians complained to King Sigismund I that the government offices in the Lithuanian and Russian provinces were distributed among the Poles. The greater part of the clergy in Lithuania at that time were Poles: the religious orders were under the jurisdiction of provincials in Poland. At the same time there was in Lithuania the greatest religious anarchy. The Polish or Polonized priests it seems were endeavoring to locate themselves in Lithuania, but were not taking the trouble to learn the Lithuanian language but simply scorned it. They preached in Polish to the Lithuanian-speaking people.* What the condition of the Catholic faith was among the people we may see from the letter

* Postilla Katholicke per Kun. M. Dauksa, Wilniui, 1599, vide preface.

of the saintly bishop of Varniai, Melchior Giedraitis, 1576 A. D., who wrote to the superior of the Jesuits asking that he send to him at least a few priests who were able to speak Lithuanian, as in the greater part of his diocese the people not only did not know the "Our Father," nor how to bless themselves, nor even to what faith they belonged.*

Protestantism, which began in the latter part of the reign of King Sigismund, spread from Poland into Lithuania, and during the time of Sigismund August, reached its highest pinnacle. Only the smaller part of the clergy in some parts of Lithuania remained Catholic. There sprung up several sects of Protestantism patronized by different magnates; each sect disturbed all the others. The people not knowing whom to believe, and not understanding the Catholic faith, in many places returned to paganism, and again started the holy fires to the pagan god Pekunas on the summits of the hills. The Polish order, the Polish speech, and the Polish customs spread in Lithuania, not because of any superior Polish culture or

* Lithuanicarum Soc. Jesu historiarum libri decem auctore Stanislos Rostovski, Wilna, 1768.

civilization; from the beginning the speech, customs, and methods of Lithuania were in no degree inferior.*

The Lithuanians, having acquired so much Slavic territory in such a short time, found it impossible to impose on the inhabitants the Lithuanian language. The whole Lithuanian class, not excepting Grand Dukes, who were to govern the conquered territories, were obliged to learn the Russian (White Russian) language, and being continually among foreigners became Slavonized. When after the transfer of the Grand Duke's court to Cracow, Lithuanian aristocracy was compelled to mix with the Poles, its members, knowing the Russian language, which is similar to Polish, and being used to foreign customs and also to the foreign language, were Polonized with greater rapidity than the Slavs or Russians; so that the conquests in Russia prepared the Lithuanian aris-

---

* The Catholic Encyclopædia, vol. 12, p. 184, states that at the time of Kazimer the Great, who died in 1370, the clergy was the only educated class in Poland. Writing of the battle of Gruenwald, the author of the article deems it necessary to mention the following: "Until then Poland had been looked upon as a semi-civilized country, where the natives were little better than savages, and culture was represented by the German clergy and colonists."

tocracy for a hastier Polonization. The first and main cause of the spread of Polonism in Lithuania was the transfer of the Grand Duke's court to Poland. With the Polonization of the aristocracy through the court of the Grand Duke, the lesser gentry at home followed their example in speech and other matters. Still further, the Polonization of the Lithuanians was advanced in the churches. The Lithuanian writer of those times, M. Dauksza, in his postilla, published in 1599, complains of the scorning of the Lithuanian language by the upper class.

To such a peril Lithuania came, while the nobility was rejoicing over their Polish privileges and the aristocracy loaned their Grand Duke to the Poles as a King. At home in Lithuania there was no ruler. The wealth of the Grand Duke, identical with that of the state, was distributed and the treasury was empty, for the taxes had been renounced in favor of the nobility. The enemy, generally Moscow, threatened Lithuania. The Polish King, though the Grand Duke of Lithuania, looked only after the interests of Poland. Instead of defending Lithuania he knew only how to advise the

Lithuanian Convention that Lithuanians instead of waging war should make one additional union with the Poles; so did Casimir, son of Jagela, on the occasion of the Moscovites occupying Novgorod, in 1478. Therefore the Grand Dukes of Lithuania were only Polish Kings; they did not reside in Lithuania, and were solicitous only about Poland. Every one of them made assignments presenting Lithuania to Poland and forced the Lithuanian magnates to sign these unions; the acknowledgment of Lithuanian delegates at the convention for the union in Parczevo, 1451, supports this.

So did even the last of those who for years wore, unworthily, the Grand Duke Vitautas's crown.

* * *

The efforts of the Poles, from the very beginning of the reign of Sigismund August, to make one more union, were not successful until in 1562 the Polonized Lithuanian and Russian small gentry formed a federation in the war camp near Vitebsk for the purpose of a complete union of Lithuania with Poland, so that they might be equal in all privileges to the Polish gentry. To satisfy their desire they abandoned the Lithuanian aristocracy and went over to the Polish side. At the Diet of Lublin in 1569, when, after lengthy discussions since January, the last loyal Lithuanians went home on the 1st of March, these conspirators against the independence of Lithuania petitioned the King that he, relying solely on their consent, affirm the union according to the wishes of the Poles. At the demands of the Poles that Podlachia and Volinia be turned over to them, the King, on the 12th of March, published a proclamation which gave these two Lithuanian provinces to Poland. The magnates of Podlachia and Volinia, Dukes Czarotoryski, Ostrozski, Visznewski, and Ostaphius Volovicz, resisted, but receiving no help from Lithuania and under penalty of being dispossessed swore their allegiance to Poland. The Lithuanian aristocracy, after breaking away from the convention, sent out a war proclamation to all Lithuania, in order to maintain by arms the independence of their country. On March 23 the Poles also announced "pospolite ruszenie," mobilization. At the demands of the Poles by the other proclamation of June 5 the King gave to Poland the provinces of Kiev and Braclav. The magnates of Lithuania, seeing that war was impossible, as the state funds from taxes had been distributed and the treasury was empty, and the Polonized gentry refusing to support war against the Poles, even threatening revolt, they sent back their delegates who on July 1 signed the union demanded by the Poles.

By this last union Lithuania and Poland were united forever. There was henceforth one ruler for both, at the same time Polish King and Grand Duke of Lithuania; one convention for common interests. The treaties with foreign states were made by both parties. But the administration, laws and courts, army, and treasury remained separate.

This union truly accomplished more than any former one. It tore away from Lithuania and gave to Poland all Russian land south of the Pripet River. By acquiring this territory Poland was more than doubled and Lithuania was reduced to the boundaries of Gedimin.

The Poles finally received from Lithuania such desirable Russian lands that they did not suggest any further union; therefore, this Lublin union was the last.

But the Lithuanians received this union as former unions. Soon after the death of King August they endeavored to secure a separate ruler, and invited Theodor, the son of John IV of Moscow, to be their Grand Duke; but the Czar promised to be ruler of Lithuania in place of his son. Then the Lithuanians withdrew. Failing to procure a separate ruler the Lithuanian Convention of Vilna sent a delegation (Christopher Radziwill) to Paris to Henry of Valois, who had been lately elected Polish King.

The Lithuanians asked him to be at the same time the Grand Duke of Lithuania, with the condition that he do not decrease the independence of Lithuania and return to her the provinces seized by Poland. From that time Lithuania and Poland always had one ruler for both.

CHAPTER IV

THE JURISTIC APPRAISEMENT OF THE BONDS BETWEEN LITHUANIAN AND POLISH STATES WHICH EXISTED BEFORE AND AFTER THE UNION OF LUBLIN

BY what legal terms of our time can we describe the bonds between Lithuania and Poland before the union of Lublin and those existing after that union? It would not suffice only to examine the words of the protocol of this or that union as well as the terms of the treaty of the Lublin union of 1569, for we have seen that the Lithuanians were not disposed to observe these unions strictly. We would do better to remark in the course of history how these agreements were observed by both sides. This will show us not only the relations desired by either side, which were written into the agreement, but the relations that existed in fact between the two states.

The Poles would like to call Lithuania a

APPRAISEMENT OF THE BONDS

Polish province. They maintain that Jagela gave Lithuania to the Poles by the pact of 1385 at Krevo. But when, soon afterward, Jagela had ascended the throne of Poland and sent his viceroy to Vilna, the Lithuanians did not acquiesce; they rose against him and proclaimed Vitautas as their ruler. Vitautas becoming Grand Duke of Lithuania, a friendly treaty was made in Ostrova, 1392, between Poland and Lithuania. This treaty we might call the alliance of our times. There was no submission of Lithuania to Poland during all the reign of Vitautas. In 1398 the Poles in the name of Hedwig had demanded from Vitautas the payment of dues as acknowledgment that Jagela had given Lithuania to Poland. Vitautas called together all the Dukes and nobility on October 2, of the same year, 1398, proclaimed himself King of independent Lithuania, and made a treaty with the Crusaders for war against Poland.

In 1401, in order to strengthen Jagela on the Polish throne after the death of his wife, Hedwig, Vitautas acknowledged him and his successors as his own successors on the Lithuanian throne by the treaty of Vilna. This meant only the promise of a real union. In 1413, when the Poles were importunate about the union, a substantial friendly treaty was made between Poland and Lithuania, by which it was agreed that both nations should elect together the rulers of their separate states. This might be taken to mean duarchy in the style of Rome under two Emperors, one ruler to have the title of King, the other that of Grand Duke, but in reality it was a shrewd move on the part of Polish politicians to elect always the same ruler for both states (Horodlo Union). During the remaining part of the reign of Vitautas this union proved to be "Confédération d'Etats," but very loose, the mutual relations of its parts being of an international character.

After the death of Vitautas, the Lithuanians elected their Grand Duke, Svitrigaila, without the Poles, and by doing this, they broke the Horodlo agreement. All the reign of Svitrigaila (1430–1432) was hostile to Poland. Sigismund, son of Kestutis, becoming Grand Duke of Lithuania in 1432, the union of 1401 between Poland and Lithuania was renewed; this meant that even the Poles themselves had repudiated the union of Horodlo. In 1440 the Lithuanians, by electing their ruler, Casimir, son of Jagela, broke the treaty with the Poles of 1432; in 1447 the Lithuanians allowed their ruler, Casimir, son of Jagela, to become also the King of Poland, and by this they agreed to a simple personal union. At his death in 1492 the union with the Poles was dissolved, the Lithuanians electing as their ruler, Alexander, and the Poles, John Albrecht. In 1499 the treaty of Horodlo was renewed for the mutual aid in wars—that of Lithuania with Moscow and that of the Poles with the Turks and Tartars. In 1501 the Poles elected the Lithuanian ruler, Alexander, as their King; again there was a personal union until the death of Alexander in 1506. When in October of that year the Lithuanians elected as their ruler the younger brother of Alexander, Sigismund, the Poles hastened to proclaim him as their King in December of the same year, and again a personal union subsisted.

During the reign of Sigismund, the Lithuanians elected his son, Sigismund August, as their Grand Duke, but not till 1544 did the ruler allow his son to take the reins of the government in Lithuania. After the death of Sigismund, in 1548, the Poles proclaimed the Lithuanian ruler, Sigismund August, as their King, and again renewed the personal union.

Therefore, we see that the signature of Jagela in 1385 at Krevo was annulled by the Lithuanians through the rising of Vitautas, and by his becoming the Grand Duke. Lithuania was always an independent and sovereign state, and did not wish to resign her sovereignty, notwithstanding the signature of a ruler who broke his fealty to the state. Until the union of Lublin, Lithuania was never incorporated with nor even vassal to Poland: not one of her rulers took an oath as vassal of King of Poland, as did the last magister of the Crusaders, Albrecht, on becoming the herzog of Prussia. Not one of them was the viceroy of the Polish King, although the Poles were demanding that Casimir, son of Jagela, become such. When the Lithuanians elected him their Grand Duke the Poles themselves were complaining that the Lithuanians broke their last treaty of 1432, and the Grand Duke Alexander sent to John Albrecht only the ordinary congratulations of a friendly neighbor, by no means a

APPRAISEMENT OF THE BONDS

vassal's submission, when the Poles elected the latter as their King. From the very election of Jagela as King of Poland until the union of Lublin the common tie between Poland and Lithuania was the same Lithuanian dynasty of Gediminas: for Poland the branch of Algirdas, and for Lithuania, at the beginning, the branch of Kestutis, in the persons of Vitautas and Sigismund, sons of Kestutis, and later, the same branch of Algirdas for both states. All these unions made between Poland and Lithuania during all those times were only friendly alliances—defensive alliances—in order that one should help another in need. Toward the end, through the efforts of Poles during the reign of several rulers, those alliances became a personal union.

* * *

What did the union of Lublin accomplish? First, it tore away from Lithuania all the southern Russians (Ukrainians), and Lithuania remained within the boundaries of Gediminas; she retained only the territories of the Lithuanians and the White Russians.

There was a change also made in regard to the legal standing of Lithuania. But regardless of the wishes of Poles Lithuania was not incorporated into Poland, even after the union of Lublin. The treaty of Lublin, as well as of other unions, in some of its parts expresses only the desires of the Poles, which were not realized later. Lithuania reserved to herself, complete and separate from Poland, a state government such as she had before the union of Lublin; a complete administration with the highest governmental institutions. This included the Convention of Lithuania which, after the union of Lublin, was called the General Convention of Lithuania, apart from the common convention of both states; her own separate code of laws (the new revised third code of the Lithuanian statute was published in 1588); her own courts; a separate army and financial system.

After the union of Lublin, therefore, Lithuania was not an autonomous province of Poland, but a sovereign and separate state as before. Therefore, after the union of Lublin we find in Lithuania all the essential characteristics of a state; a separate territory under the high dominion of the government of Lithuania and even the rights of the international relations (jus foederum ac legationum).

APPRAISEMENT OF THE BONDS

After the death of Sigismund August the Lithuanians sent a delegation to Moscow asking the Czar's son to be their ruler, and again they sent another delegation to France inviting Henry of Valois to their throne. Even the convention at Lublin recognized the independence of Lithuania from Poland by separating from Lithuania and joining to Poland, Podlachia, Volinia, Podolia, Kiev, and Braclav, up to that time Lithuanian territories. This would not have been necessary if Lithuania had become a Polish province, as after the union of Lublin Kiev and Volinia became. This convention of Lublin acknowledged the fact of a separate allegiance to Lithuania and Poland. On the transference of these provinces into Polish hands, when the union was being consummated, the inhabitants were obliged to take an oath of allegiance to Poland; this was demanded expressly to show the transition from the Lithuanian allegiance to a Polish allegiance—only states, never provinces, have a right to demand the allegiance of the inhabitants of a territory. That Lithuania was not an autonomous province of Poland but a state quite separate from Poland is shown by the very origin of the government of Lithuania over her territory. Her territory and the power of governing it Lithuania did not acquire from Poland, as Poland did not possess them previously; but all this Lithuania as a sovereign state possessed before the union of Lublin by her own right, and in entering a convention with Poland she reserved to herself that territory and jurisdiction over it. Therefore we see at the unfortunate Lublin union that the Lithuanian delegates, compelled to sign the treaty of the union, on their knees begged their Grand Duke that he should not destroy the independence nor tarnish the honor of his own native land, Lithuania. If Lithuania was a sovereign state before the union of Lublin and the Lithuanians did not wish to renounce her independence, then the question is, how could she become a Polish province, as Poles had never conquered her?

Until the fall of Poland, therefore, the Lithuanians considered themselves as constituting a separate nation, the subjects not of Poland but of the supreme Lithuanian Government, expressing the will of the nation. Before the actual subjection of Lithuania to Russia (in 1794)

APPRAISEMENT OF THE BONDS 47

"the General Confederacy of the Grand Duchy of Lithuania" speaks of "the will of the Lithuanian nation." Where is the province to be found that expresses the will of the nation? The foreign diplomats even at the end of the eighteenth century knew very well that Lithuania was not a part of Poland, but an altogether separate state. Prince V. N. Repnin, former Russian ambassador in Warsaw, writes to Dimitri Troschinski, a high Russian official, in regard to territories acquired by Russia after the partition of Poland-Lithuania: "Lithuania should remain separate from Poland in her government, in her domain and organization, as she was before, a separate state from Poland."

* * *

What really was the bond between Poland and Lithuania from the union of Lublin until the fall of these two states? All that time both states having their complete separate governments had in common only one ruler with the double title—that of King of Poland and Grand Duke of Lithuania. Each ruler was elected for life at the common convention of both states. The treaties of these sovereign states touching the affairs of both states had to be made by both in common. General conventions of the delegates of both states were called together in common to pass on the common affairs of both states; from 1673 they were convened alternately, first in Lithuania then in Poland.

From what has been said we see that Lithuania, a sovereign state, then in a personal union with Poland, joined Poland as an equal at the union of Lublin; so the relations between them, even after the Lublin union, were those of co-ordination not of subordination, of equality of rights. The bonds between states enjoying equal rights sometimes may be very loose and temporary, as, for instance, an alliance for a certain stated time. Here in the relations of Lithuania and Poland we see a stronger bond—a community of certain state organs and interests—but this bond never became the bond of a so-called federal state (état Fédéral). Two bordering states did not become one organized partnership, with a government exercising its constitution and its rights over the territory of both, each of which delegated to it certain of their sovereign rights,

APPRAISEMENT OF THE BONDS

as in the case of Switzerland's Eidgenossenschaft since 1848 or the German Empire since 1871. Lithuania and Poland did not possess a new government created by the union superior to the government of each. Therefore their mutual relations were of an international character. In them we find only the community of certain organs in each state, in this case in one physical person, exercising the sovereignty of both states—one ruler.

But here this personal union was not temporal—accidental—as sometimes happens through rights of heredity converging in one person to form a personal union in the strict sense. In the case of Lithuania and Poland the union was effected by agreement and in time by long enduring custom—a stable union with the same ruler for both states forever, and therefore a real union.

The union of Lithuania and Poland fully resembles the bond of Austria and Hungary of the recent times. Austria-Hungary by the Constitution of 1867 had one ruler, the Emperor of Austria and King of Hungary; he was vested with the exterior sovereignty of both states; he was also the chief commander of the common army. In Lithuania and Poland there was one ruler, the King of Poland and the Grand Duke of Lithuania, but Lithuania and Poland, as well as Austria and Hungary, had a separate government and separate laws. On account of the common interests of both states Austria-Hungary has delegations from both parliaments; Lithuania and Poland had the common convention of the delegates of both states to look after the common affairs.

* * *

So Lithuania after the Lublin union remained a separate state, but remained in a real union with Poland until December of 1795, when she was finally divided between Russia and Prussia. The political history of Lithuania after the Lublin union is closely connected with the history of Poland. The period from the Lublin union till the fall of both extends over more than two hundred years. In 1572 the male Jagelon line of the dynasty of Gediminas ended, and in 1772 there was the first division of Lithuania-Poland. From 1572 until 1673, if we omit Henry of Valois, who was in Cracow only five months, only one man not Lithuanian, Stephan Batory, was the King and Grand

APPRAISEMENT OF THE BONDS

Duke.* The other rulers were from the other branch of the same Lithuanian dynasty. The first male from the female Jagelon line was one of the Vazas, of Sweden, and after them came Michael Wisniowiecki, who is considered as of the other line of Gediminas. Of the others, the first was John Sobieski (1674) and the last was August Poniatowski (1764) both Poles; and between them are two Germans, the Saxon Kurfuersts, August II and Frederick August III, not counting the Pole Stanislaus Leszczinski, who was proclaimed King and supported for five years by Charles XII during wars with Sweden.

After the Napoleonic wars and the Congress of Vienna the fate of the Lithuanian nation was determined as follows: All the territories of the Letts and the greater part of the Lithuanian territory was apportioned to Russia and only the smaller part of Lithuania at the mouth of Niemen, toward the sea beyond the Pregel River, was left to Prussia.

* He was elected King on the condition that he marry Anna Jagelon, sister of August, who was elected Queen before him.

CHAPTER V

THE CAUSES OF THE DOWNFALL OF THE POLISH (AND WITH IT THE LITHUANIAN) STATE; THE UNION WITH LITHUANIA IS THE TRUE REASON FOR THE GROWTH OF THE POLISH NATION AND STATE, BUT, AT THE SAME TIME, THE CAUSE OF INTERNAL ANARCHY AND THE DOWNFALL OF THAT STATE

THE cause of the partition of Poland and Lithuania by their neighbors was the same that led Lithuania to the Lublin union, the weakening almost to extinction of the power of the state at home and abroad. The Poles, before forcing upon Lithuania the privileges of the nobility, had extended these privileges beforehand at home and continually invented new privileges. The Grand Dukes and Kings, continually renouncing prerogatives of their power in behalf of the gentry, finally left to themselves no power either over the gentry or over the other people depending on gentry. As regards the power of the ruler in Lithuania and Poland we observe a counterpart of what happened contemporaneously in Germany with the imperial power, with the difference that fortunately for Germany the prerogatives of the supreme power there were surrendered to the governors of provinces by heredity; to the Kurfuersts, to the Herzogs, and the Grafs; as if in Lithuania the powers of the Grand Duke had been distributed to the smaller Dukes possessing the rights of heredity. In Lithuania and Poland the prerogatives of supreme power were divided among all the members of the nobility possessing estates; every one of these rich noblemen on his estates was equal to the German Kurfuerst, Herzog, or Graf. Finally, only a shadow of royal power was left to the Polish King and Grand Duke of Lithuania—no more power than was possessed by his picture hanging on the wall. The legislative power of the convention was destroyed by the introduction of "liberum veto." The army to defend the borders of the state consisted of the gentry called together by "pospolite ruszenie"—the mobilization. But this army could not remain in mobilization more than three months and could not be led over the border more than three miles. It is evident that there could be no discipline in such an army; often, as soon as it had collected it dispersed without action. The handful of a regular hired army was independent of the King, and very often collected its pay by force. In one word, there was but a nominal central government. There was a King, a Grand Duke, and the Convention, but their action was paralyzed—reduced to zero; there existed practically no executive power whatever; the defense of the state from the external foe was practically nil. The only way to accomplish something for the welfare of the land was by the so-called confederacy of the gentry, a kind of an agreement for a definite aim. The convention of such a confederacy made its resolutions by the majority vote. But a confederacy was dangerous; it always resulted in civil war; against one confederacy there often arose another in complete opposition. Therefore, generally, the government could not have recourse to it. A French publicist of those times, C. C. de Rulhière, called this liberty, these laws, and the government of which the Poles were boasting, barbaric: "Ainsi se sont perpétués depuis un temps immémorial jusqu'à notre âge, et chez une nation justement célèbre, la liberté, les gouvernements et les lois des barbares." *

The statesmen of Lithuania, long before the downfall of their country, fully understood the perniciousness of those Polish privileges and condemned them, but they were unable to free themselves from them. We have testimony to this effect in the Confederation of Vilna of November 29, 1700, which was signed by all the highest officials of the Supreme Lithuanian Government, from the Lithuanian Chancellor, Duke Charles Radizwill, to the Supreme Commander of the Armies of Lithuania (The Great Hetman of Lithuania) Duke Michael Korybut Wisniowiecki. By this document the magnates of Lithuania renounced and condemned the liberties brought from Poland to Lithuania and wished to return to the absolute power of the Grand Duke as it existed in the times of Gediminas and Vitautas; they declared they were convinced that the Polish liberties were leading to the perdition. But here, as in the times of the Lublin union, what was evidently pernicious to well-educated and broad-minded

* Histoire de l'anarchie de Pologne et du démembrement ... par Claude Carloman de Rulhière, 1807.

magnates was desired by the egoistic mob of uneducated, short-sighted small gentry of the provinces.

When the power was scattered in Germany among Herzogs and counts—not an ordinary gentry (Rittern), but the rulers of provinces possessing rights of succession (Landesherren)—there were among them ambitious and able men who, enlarging gradually their wealth and influence, could create centres that in time would unite again the whole wide-spread state and nation. In Lithuania and Poland the reverse happened. In Germany the power of the state was transferred to Landesherren. In Lithuania and Poland that power was simply destroyed. Moreover, the magnates, estate owners, were only the private possessors of real estate, not the rulers of provinces, not Landesherren. There were no centres that could unite the whole land. Therefore both countries, Lithuania and Poland, collapsed into anarchy. Poland, abusing the weakened and half-dead government of Lithuania, in 1569 at Lublin broke away and separated by force the provinces of Volynia and Ukraine; the remainder of Lithuania she did not make her province, but merely forced her into a union, only because she herself was weak as a military power and did not wish to drive the Lithuanians into war. In 1772, 1793, and 1795 the same thing was repeated by the neighboring states, not only in regard to Lithuania but also in regard to Poland, with this difference only—that the negotiations about the unions were unnecessary. With strong armies to back their decisions strong neighbors did not fear the opposition in Lithuania and Poland; they simply divided them amongst themselves. The titles upon which successful despoilers took the Polish provinces are striking; they are neither more nor less just than those titles upon which Poland took, at the Lublin union, the Lithuanian provinces, Volynia, Kiev, and others. Prussia and Austria, relying on old meaningless titles, claimed that they were taking back what "justly" belonged to them. But the most adroit, perhaps, were the declarations of Catherine: "Après les dépenses considérables en hommes et en argent qu'a coutées à l'empire de Russie son assistance à la Pologne pour la sauver de la fureur de ses propres citoyens ... il doit paraître bien modéré que sa Majesté se borne . . . à se procurer la réparation de dommage" (C. C. de Rulhière). They divided among themselves the Polish provinces because they wished to save Poland from the Poles!

The cause of the downfall of the Lithuanian state, of the misery, of the decrease, and of the weakening of the nation itself is evident. It was association with the Poles. The identification of the Grand Duke with the King of Poland; the distribution of Polish privileges among the gentry; the influence of the Poles in Lithuania through a King's court, through Polish privileges, and through the Polish church and the schools in Lithuania under its jurisdiction, notably the University of Cracow before the Lublin union, and later the Polish Academy at Vilna: These were the means by which the governmental power of the state in Lithuania was weakened. The higher classes of the nation were Polonized, and by the spread of Polonism the patriotism of the nobility and the spirit of nationality was demoralized; this led the Lithuanians to the Lublin union. From that time the influence of the Poles spread rapidly in Lithuania. The majority of the gentry accepted the Polish language. The greater part of the priesthood, already Polish, now became a powerful factor in Polonizing the people. Lithuanian patriotism, Lithuanian nationality was mixed with the Polish. This became a by-word: "gente Lithuanus, natione Polonus." The Polish speech among Lithuanians became the speech of the educated class. There was real danger that the Lithuanian state would become a Polish province and that the Lithuanian nation would perish with the dying out of the Lithuanian language. On the other hand, Poland became a great world power only after the union with Lithuania. The small Polish nation grew big by the union with Lithuania. By the Polonization of the Lithuanian gentry and educated classes the power of the Polish literary, artistic, and upper classes, also the influence of Polish culture, greatly increased. The names of men of Lithuanian origin adorn Polish history and literature, names like Mickiewicz, Kosciuszko. Lithuanian magnates, such as Radziwills, Pac'es, Sapieha's, and the Czartoryski's, the princes of the Gediminas family now became Polish magnates. Their wealth was helping Polish culture and Polish interests. This is the reason the Poles so highly honor the "Jagellonians" and cling to the Lithuanians, so that when the Lithuanians of our time desire to realize their own independent destiny the Poles per fas et nefas would retain them in their care. It seems to the Poles that the Lithuanians by fate itself are destined to belong to them, so that they may grow and become great on the ruins of the Lithuanian nation.

Nevertheless this union with Lithuania and this invitation to a Lithuanian dynasty to rule over them, which contributed so much toward the growth and fame of the Polish nation, was the real cause of the downfall of their state. A foreign dynasty invited to rule by the nobility felt its dependence upon them and did not feel as secure upon the throne as if it had been a native Polish dynasty. We see even in Jagela's hands a weak kingly power. He and his successors felt that they reigned by the grace of the nobility; that this nobility might not choose their son to the succession. Therefore every one of them at the beginning of his reign, to insure the throne to his son, diminished the power and the wealth of the office and oppressed the lower classes for the benefit of the nobility by giving privileges until there remained only a shadow of a King's authority. Among the nobility there sprung up magnates equal to feudal Dukes of other countries. The authority of the King collapsed altogether, and each of the magnates looked out for his own benefit; they began wars among themselves or rose against the King; and during the election of a King they began to call in the aid of foreign governments.

This anarchy was increased by the unfortunate union with Lithuania, a foreign nation several times larger than Poland. The Poles continually endeavored to incorporate Lithuania with Poland, and the Lithuanians during all this time were opposing these efforts; the history of these centuries records continual breaking of the unions by the Lithuanians:* the open siding with Poland's foes in war-

* In 1655 the Government of Lithuania made a treaty with Sweden against Poland during the latter's war with Charles Gustav; Janusz and Boguslav Radziwills endeavored to separate Lithuania from Poland; Prince Sapieha and his party waged war against the King in 1700; the Russians of eastern provinces in the wars with Moscow sided against Poland and joined the state of Moscow.

time; religious strife between the Orthodox and Catholics; such antagonism between the nationality of the Lithuanians and the Poles, that even such Lithuanians as had adopted the Polish language, until very recent times, endeavored to accentuate their Lithuanianism.* Therefore the united Lithuanian-Polish state, although in its time the largest in Europe, never showed such a great power abroad as its size warranted; and later on, through mutual strife and anarchy, it gradually grew weaker, until it finally collapsed.

So the union of Poland with Lithuania led both to anarchy and to final collapse.

*Vide British Review, February, 1915. Autonomy of Poland and Lithuania. J. Gabrys Lietuviu-Lenku Unija. The Lithuanian Polish Union.

CHAPTER VI

THE SURVIVAL OF THE NATIONAL CONSCIOUSNESS OF THE LITHUANIANS UP TO THE PRESENT DAY THROUGH THE PRESERVATION OF THEIR OWN LANGUAGE, TRADITIONS, AND THE EXPRESSION OF THAT CONSCIOUSNESS IN THEIR LITERATURE; THE RISE AND EXPANSION AMONG THE LITHUANIANS OF THE IDEA OF NATIONAL INDEPENDENCE FROM DANGEROUS FOREIGN INFLUENCE; THE PRESENT CULTURAL AND ECONOMIC GROWTH OF THE NATION

AT the end of the eighteenth century the Lithuanian state collapsed; but the Lithuanian nation, although very badly impaired and in the run of centuries decreased by more than half, did not cease to exist. For the state is not the nation. The state is only an institution of a nation; that institution without which the nation can live long, even growing larger and stronger, as did the nomadic Israelites before the occupation of Canaan. A nation can be defined as a composite entity with customs, language, and a conscious spirit by which it conceives of itself as having a being distinct from that of any other similar group of humanity. No one will say that after the fall of the Polish state, even after the last insurrection of the Poles in 1863, when the Russian Government abolished the last rights of Polish autonomy, there was no longer a Polish nation.

There is to-day, as in the case of the Poles, a Lithuanian nation; and there are many other nations which as yet are not actual states, but have their language, their traditions, and a consciousness of their distinctness from other groups of humanity and their peculiar spiritual life. A state is, as we said, a national institution without which a civilized nation cannot easily exist. A state is like the home of a nation, a guarantee of her self-independence; without it a nation, although it exists, is oppressed by others, robbed and often destroyed; and serving a stranger, frequently forced to defend its very existence, it finds it difficult to achieve anything for the benefit of humanity.

The life of a nation manifests itself in its traditions, which again are preserved in the national language and reveal themselves in its literature. Given a language and a literature, no nation can be considered to be dead or non-existent, for she herself is conscious of her existence. But if it is not also a state, another nation which compelled it to belong to it can oppress it, but cannot say that it as a nation does not exist.

Nearly all the literature of the European nations, with the exception of the Greeks and Latins, began after the adoption of Christianity. Lithuania was the last European nation to accept Christianity. There is evidence in pre-historic times that the Runic writings were known in Lithuania. After the founding of the Lithuanian state the Latin language was used in the Grand Duke's office in transactions with western Europe, and the Slavonian church language in dealings with the Russian Dukes. In 1529 the code of Lithuanian laws was published in the Slavic language.

The first books printed in the Lithuanian language, which were of purely religious type, appeared in the middle of the sixteenth century. They were written by the clergy and answered their purposes; for the priests, having to deal with people that understood no language but the Lithuanian, had to use this language in their books. Books of the belles-lettres and worldly poetry could not be found at this period, for few of the wealthy people were educated in western Europe and they became interested in Latin and various other languages of the West. The first book publishers had established themselves with the higher educational institutions. There had been since 1544 a university at Königsberg, which was the first in the territory of the Lithuanian nation. Here the first Lithuanian books were printed.

Two editions of a small catechism in the Prussian language were published in 1545, and in 1547 M. Vaitkunas, pastor of Ragnit, published the first book in the Lithuanian language containing a short catechism, the first elementary reading, and some hymns. The book was dedicated to the Grand Duke of Lithuania. Luther's Enchiridion, or the Smaller Catechism, was published in the Prussian language in Königsberg in 1561; in 1579 the same work was translated into Lithuanian by B. Villentas, the pastor of Königsberg.

From 1578 we have evidence of official Lithuanian writing.

In the meantime in Vilna, in 1566, the second edition of the Lithuanian Statute was published, and in 1588 the third edition, both in the Slavic language. The third edition was translated into the Polish language—a sign of early Polonizing of the higher classes of Lithuania.

About the year 1580 J. Bretkunas, a Lithuanian pastor of Labguva, later of Königsberg, translated the whole Bible.

The Hymn Book, by Bretkunas, was published in 1589; in 1591 his Postilla (sermons).

In 1612 L. Sengstock, pastor of Königsberg, published his Hymnal. About the middle of the seventeenth century the Prussian Lithuanians had a conspicuous writer, D. Kleinis, pastor of Tilsit. In 1653 he published Grammatica Lithuanica; in 1666 he published also in Königsberg the Hymn Book, one of the best books of the kind in the Lithuanian language. It was republished in 1685, 1705, 1869. In 1872 it was revised by Fr. Kurszatis. Up to the present time it is the best of Lutheran hymnals and prayer-books in Lithuanian.

In the latter part of the sixteenth century Duke M. Radziwill founded a school with the

Calvin Church in Vilna, and Birze, and the printing establishment at Nesviez. During the Lublin Diet in 1569 the Jesuits obtained permission to come to Lithuania, and in the second year after that they opened their college at Vilna, which in 1578 was changed to an academy, adding to it their printing establishment. In Vilna, the heart of Lithuania, a second publishing house arose for the printing of Lithuanian books—Catholic as well as Protestant.

In 1595 appeared the Catechism of Ledesma, translated by Michael Dauksas, a Samogitian prelate.

In 1599, in Vilna, appeared Postilla, by the same M. Dauksas.

In 1600 in Vilna was published the Lithuanian Postilla (Calvinist), by Jacob Morkunas, a newly revised edition. When the first edition was printed is not known.

In 1605 the Catechism of Ledesma was published in the eastern Lithuanian dialect.

At the beginning of the seventeenth century a famous writer, Reverend Constant Sirvidas, a Jesuit, a professor of the Academy of Vilna and a Lithuanian preacher of Saint John's

NATIONAL CONSCIOUSNESS

Church, labored in Vilna. Of his books the following were published in Vilna: in 1629 his Book of Sermons; in 1644, Lenten Sermons, Clavis linguæ Lituanicæ, a grammar; a dictionary, Dictionarium trium linguarum, Lithuanian, Latin, and Polish—only the fourth edition of 1677 remains, the date of the first edition is not known.

In 1737, in Vilna, appeared Typis Collegii Academici Soc. Jesu Universitas linguarum lituanicæ in principali Ducatus ejusdem grammaticis legibus circumscripta.

In 1677, in Vilna, the Lithuanian translation of the catechism of Cardinal Bellarmin was published.

Adalbert Kojalowcz, a professor and rector of the Academy of Vilna, wrote (1) Historiæ Lituaniæ Pars prior to 1387, which was printed at Danzig in 1650, and (2) Pars altera, printed at Antwerp in 1669.

In 1705, in Vilna, the book of Gospels and Epistles was published. It was reprinted in 1711, 1750, 1803. This was the best Lithuanian book of the kind.

It is noteworthy that the Lithuanian language in the books printed in Königsberg, as well as in Vilna, is grammatically perfect in phraseology, the selection of words fitting accurately to their meaning, etc., which shows that the Lithuanian language was used in literature a century previous to this.

With the weakening of Protestantism in Vilna the publication of Protestant Lithuanian books in Vilna ceased.

In the middle of the seventeenth century the city of Keidany became the centre of Protestant activity, the seat of the Calvinistic Synod. In 1653, in Keidany, the book, Lithuanian Prayer Book, dedicated to Duke Janusz Radziwill, was published. In 1553, also in Keidany, Summa or the Explanation of Gospels was published, and in 1653 A Prayer Book for All Year Around.

From 1657 to 1666, through the efforts of the Calvinistic Synod of Keidany, the Lithuanian edition of the Bible was printed in London.

In 1701 the Calvins of Keidany published in Königsberg the New Testament in Lithuanian.

In Prussia, in the eighteenth century, the government assisted in a revision toward uniformity in the prayer-book. In 1719 Doctor H.

Lysius, at the order of the government, published a small catechism of Martin Luther.

More difficulties were encountered with the hymnals, the work upon them by the Prussian Lithuanian clergy being carried over the greater part of the eighteenth century. After several revisions the consistory of eastern Prussia finally published, in 1791, in Königsberg, a Hymnal containing five hundred and forty-two hymns. This was revised and republished many times later.

Along with these religious works there appeared in Prussia two well-known writers, Philip Ruhig, pastor of Valterkiemis, who in 1747 published the Lithuanian dictionary, and Kr. Donelaitis, the first Lithuanian poetical genius. Among his productions is a great poem, Metu Laikai, The Seasons of the Year, in hexameter.

His work describes the life of the Lithuanian peasant at the end of the eighteenth century just as Mickiewicz's Pan Tadeusz, written in Polish, tells of the life of the Polonized Lithuanian gentry from the beginning of the nineteenth century; each of these works is complementary to the other; but the Mickiewicz picture of the Polonized Lithuanian gentry is idealized and adorned in accordance with Polish patriotism. Throughout, the best side is presented. The picture of the life of the gentry as a whole is incomplete; their relations with their bondsmen are hardly mentioned; but the form and style of the whole work is perfect. Donelaitis's picture of the life of the peasants is altogether real, even in respect of their uncultured language and their unrefined behavior.

In the nineteenth century L. Reza, who died in 1840, published Donelaitis's poems, and in 1824 the complete edition of the Old and New Testaments. In the same year he published Æsop's Fables, and in the following year a collection of Lithuanian Songs (Daina) with their German translations. Immanuel Kant, the great German philosopher, expressed high admiration for the folk-lore contained therein. F. Kurszatis, who died in 1884, revised and published in 1854 the Lithuanian edition of the New Testament and the Hymnal, as well as the prayer-book for the Prussian army, the catechism for the schools, the German Lithuanian Dictionary, and the Lithuanian

Grammar in German. From 1849 to 1880 he published in Königsberg the newspaper Keleivis, which was well liked by the Lithuanians.

* * *

In the nineteenth century almost the entire Lithuanian nation, arrested by the unfortunate political tendencies of the Lithuanian Government, beginning with Jagela and the unions with the Poles, finds itself within the boundaries of the Russian Empire. Only a smaller part of the Lithuanians, living at the mouth of the Niemen toward the Baltic Sea as far south as the river Pregel, belonged to Prussia. On the downfall of the states of Lithuania and Poland, Polish patriotism first expanded and intensified, so affecting the Polonized strata of the Lithuanian nation as to urge them to further Polonization. The Vilna educational district, with the University of Vilna and the Polish schools throughout Lithuania, and two Polish uprisings against Russia in 1831 and 1863 greatly advanced the vehement Polonization of Lithuania. In 1803 Czartoryski, the Polish aristocrat, a descendant of the Grand Dukes of Lithuania, was appointed president of the educational district of Vilna, which extended over almost the whole of Lithuania. He transformed the Jesuit Academy of Vilna into a university, and in connection with it also established a grand seminary for the priests. He ordered the monasteries to maintain elementary schools, about forty in number, throughout Lithuania. All these schools were Polish and were under the jurisdiction of the Polonized university; they systematically conducted the Polonization of Lithuania. The University of Vilna, with these other schools, was abolished by the Russian Government only after the Polish uprising in 1830–1831. The work of Polonization of Lithuania was continued by the churches, as before, and by the University of Vilna and its schools. In many parishes the Lithuanian tongue was replaced by the Polish. Priests ignorant of the Lithuanian language were intentionally sent to Lithuanian-speaking parishes, and those speaking Lithuanian were sent to Russian-speaking churches. Each uprising of the Poles was the cause of greater intensification of Polish patriotism, and drew more and more Lithuanians to the Polish side.

Nevertheless, the Lithuanian national spirit

could not die as long as the language of the nation lived. The glorious Lithuanian national traditions were cherished even by the already Polonized Lithuanians of the upper classes. In the first part of the nineteenth century, and later, we find a whole line of able Lithuanian writers who wrote in Polish, such as Mickiewicz, J. I. Kraszewski, Narbutt, Kondratowicz, Ign. Chodzko, Odyniec, Mary Radziewicz. Some of their works only belong to Polish literature because they were written in the Polish language: their ideas and purport served to revive the Lithuanian national consciousness. This was the case with Mickiewicz's Grazyna and Konrad Wallenrod; Kraszewski's Plaint of Vitolis, Mindove, Vitautas's Battles, and The History of Lithuania, and Narbutt's History of Lithuania, etc.

In the nineteenth century Lithuanian writers increase greatly in number. And after 1869, when slavery was abolished by the Russian Government, a great number of peasants' sons joined the ranks of Lithuanian writers.

We have poems written in those times by Dionysius Poszka, Reverend Anthony Drazdauskas and Reverend Simon Staneviczus, rector of the ecclesiastical seminary at Varniai, etc.

In 1832, in Prussia, the first Lithuanian periodical was published by Fr. Kalkis.

The period of 1840 to 1870, of Daukantas (1864), and Bishop Valanczauskis (1875), was a golden one for the Lithuanian literature. Both wrote and published many a Lithuanian book. About this time L. Ivinskis, Dovidaviczus, Tatare, and Bishop A. Baranauskas began to write, and Reverend A. Juszkeviczus published a collection of 5,600 folk-songs, etc.

In 1847 L. Ivinskis began to publish his yearly almanacs, so famous among Lithuanians.

In 1854 a famous linguist, Schleicher, publishes in Prague his great work, The Lithuanian Grammar (in German).

In 1880, in Tilsit, Prussia, the Lithuanian Literary Society was organized, whose activity encouraged so much the educated Lithuanians in Prussian and Russian Lithuania to return to the use of the language of their fathers.

In March of 1883 there begins to appear in Ragnit, later in Tilsit, Prussia, the monthly, Auszra, or The Dawn, to voice the patriotism of the new era in Lithuania. The appear-

NATIONAL CONSCIOUSNESS

ance of Auszra is the starting-point of the Lithuanian national consciousness, and of the organized national attempt for liberation from injurious foreign influences.

Some call this period the revival. The term is not strictly correct. The consciousness of the Lithuanian nationalism and individuality had never ceased to exist. The nation therefore was not asleep. But national consciousness was passive; the nation did not defend itself. There had been no idea that foreign influences were dangerous. But in the middle of the nineteenth century, when the Polonization had reached its highest mark in Lithuania and the real peril of the extinction of the Lithuanian language became apparent, the more intelligent minds foresaw the danger to the nation itself. Then did the nation understand that it had been heretofore in a false position and energetic persons began the work of organizing the nation. The movement started with the defense of the Lithuanian language and later concerned itself with the other abandoned interests of the nation. Before, there was passive consciousness in the nation, now there was full understanding; and to ward off the danger the political programme was drawn up, positive action outlined, and organization perfected.

Auszra appears in Prussia, because after the Polish insurrection of 1863 the Lithuanian publications were forbidden in Russia. Only after forty years of hardest unequal struggle of the nation in behalf of the press was the ban on the press lifted by Russia in 1904. The martyrs of the Lithuanian national ideal had suffered exile and imprisonment in Siberia and other distant Russian provinces.

We have seen that the political union with the Poles greatly injured the Lithuanian nation; almost the entire upper class adopted the Polish speech; entire districts of the territory inhabited by Lithuanians in the south and east became Polonized or Russianized. Nevertheless the Lithuanian idea—the national consciousness—remained unimpaired to the last. When, after long bondage, there sprang up numerous Lithuanian educated men from the peasant stock, these would not adopt a foreign tongue. Turning to a pure national ideal they counted every foreign influence over their nation as dangerous, and began to urge entire rejection of Polonism; though many who had adopted the Polish language before began to renounce their Lithuanian nationalism, standing with the Polish nation and proclaiming themselves Poles.

Since 1883, however, Lithuanian literature, and with it the new national ideal, spread with unbounded force through Lithuania. As time went on new poets, writers of fiction, scientific writers, philologists, and other writers appeared.

During the Russian revolution of 1905 the national consciousness in Lithuania was so strong and wide-spread throughout the land that it was possible to call a national convention from all parts of Lithuania. This national convention was held on December 4 and 5, 1905. It was there resolved by the district and county conventions to remove from Lithuania all Russian office-holders and to introduce a Lithuanian government everywhere.*

The resolutions of this national convention

* During the twenty years previous to the lifting of the ban against Lithuanian literature imposed by the Russian Government (1886–1905), five Lithuanian publishing houses flourished in the United States. Through the efforts of J. Panksitis, D. T. Boczkowski, A. M. Milukas, A. Olszewski, Lithuanian Alliance of America, and Society of Lithuanian Patriots, over four hundred works were published, including masterpieces of Lithuanian literature and translations of the classic of the English and other literatures.

were disseminated in all Lithuania immediately after the return of the delegates from the convention. Only by the proclamation of martial law and with the help of the army did the Russian Government subdue this movement of the Lithuanians. But although the old order of the government was resumed, more freedom remained in the land; the Lithuanian language was still used in the schools and in some lower government institutions. Lithuanians were permitted to take governmental offices in Lithuania.

Lately, after the revolution of 1905 and after the national convention at Vilna, the Lithuanian nation, enjoying more liberty, rose considerably, both spiritually and economically.

The national consciousness and the desire of full independence mastered the entire nation. Literary and economic societies were founded; private, elementary, and high schools were established, as well as banks of credit and trade exchanges. Farming associations, co-operative trade associations, educational, scientific, and artists' societies were founded. Lately, the Lithuanian nation has grown considerably in power, educationally and materially, and has perfected its cultural and political life.

CHAPTER VII

PRESENT NATIONAL ASPIRATIONS OF THE LITHUANIANS: THE POLITICAL UNITY AND INDEPENDENCE OF ALL PARTS OF THE LITHUANIAN NATION NOW UNDER DIFFERENT GOVERNMENTS (RUSSIAN AND GERMAN); FREEDOM FROM FOREIGN INFLUENCES; THE PRESERVATION OF ONE AND SOLE LITHUANIAN LANGUAGE AS THE NATIONAL TONGUE; RELATIONS WITH THE POLES, WHITE RUSSIANS, AND LETTS

WE have learned of the past; let us endeavor to examine the present aims of the Lithuanian nation. Now the Lithuanian nation is alive, self-conscious, and eager to be completely free of foreign tutelage, to become independent, to realize itself. The ideal of every nation is the political union of all parts of the nation in a single independent state. Political unions forcing different nations to combine into one state are mistakes or misfortunes; they bring one or several of those united nations to destruction. The peril of such unions is demonstrated to us by history. Even when populous and powerful nations receive into their state large foreign elements and assimilate them by force or by lapse of time and the influence of life, they themselves degenerate into a different nation and lose their former character and being. The Latin nation which founded the worldwide state of Rome perished by mixture with the conquered nations, and degenerated into several new and previously non-existent nations; neither French, nor Italians, nor Roumanians are the old Latin nation that founded Rome. The Bohemian nation has been for a long time in a union of German nations, has continuously accepted on her throne a succession of German princes, and finally entered wholly into a personal union with Austria in 1526. But what advantage did she gain? She completely lost her kingdom and her independence. Her territory, that formerly had embraced Bohemia, Moravia, and Silesia, now is half Germanized and even divided between several German states; eventually she found herself almost without hope of ever regaining her independence. The same thing happened to Lithuania. The error of Algirdas with relation to the Russians and the still greater error of Jagela with relation to the Poles led us to the same consequences as the Bohemians arrived at. If after this war our nation is not permitted to unite and to organize as a state, in the course of future ages there may remain only a small remnant of us, without hope, as in the case of the Eastern nations: the Copts of Egypt, the Syrians, Phœnicians, and Assyrians. Denationalization of the foreign nations received into a state is being accomplished in the interests either of the dynasty or of the ruling classes of the compound state for the alleged strengthening of the state, which these classes or dynasties consider as their property. Formerly the nations that found themselves in a foreign state were always denationalized. The same fate will befall such nations in the future. And the Lithuanian nation, to be free from such a danger, must necessarily separate itself from the foreign nations and organize its own state. Therefore the well-defined aim of our patriots should be not the rebuilding of the Lithuania that existed in the past, not the union with other nations, whether Poles, White Russians, or Russians, but the uniting of all parts of the territory inhabited by the Lithuanian people which are now distributed among the neighboring states, and out of this united territory, the making of a new Lithuanian state free of foreign influences.

It is absolutely necessary that Lithuanians renounce all those parts of their former states which are inhabited by pure White Russians or Poles; but all the territory inhabited by the Lithuanians must be united. From the future Lithuania should be separated those districts that are Lithuanian in a broad ethnographical way; where there formerly lived people of the same Lithuanian race using the Lithuanian language, but who a very long time ago adopted the White Russian or Polish language, as, for instance, the territories of Jacvingi to the south from the Niemen; or the eastern countries of the government of Vilna, where there is no wide area using the Lithuanian language, and therefore no hope of return to the Lithuanian language of their forefathers. The more of those denationalized sections that we receive into a Lithuanian state the greater White Russian influence they will exercise on the pure Lithuanian nation. We must satisfy ourselves with the borderlands where the Lithuanian language is used widely, if not entirely, wherever these borderlands are absolutely necessary for the natural and strategical frontiers of the state. The state should include not only the ethnographic parts of Lithuania that belonged till lately to Russia, but also the terrain at the mouth of the Niemen, now under Prussia, where the Lithuanian language is used. Control of the mouth is essential to the future Lithuanian state, because the Niemen is the only navigable river that flows through Lithuania; the mouth of the Niemen is Lithuania's only exit to the sea and to all the world; and as the regions about it are inhabited by Lithuanians, *to take it from Lithuania would be maliciously to shut off Lithuania from communication with the world.*

The Lithuanian state should comprise the territories inhabited by the Lithuanian race for thousands of years. If there are some stretches with inhabitants who accepted other languages, there remain between them other stretches where the Lithuanian language of their forefathers is preserved; and these very same people, even though they use a different language, are by race and blood Lithuanians, as much so as those of the centre of Lithuanian territory. They will not imperil the true Lithuanian nationalism; but without those borderlands Lithuania cannot possess any satisfactory natural frontiers to her national territory.

Let us by no means form a nation of many languages. To do that would be to take the road to disorder, denationalization, and final national annihilation. A nation with several languages can exist only through one common religion, for which it is persecuted by others; or through one government that has developed in the course of ages: as soon as this government falls, it is impossible to gather together the parts that speak different languages. Let us Lithuanians rather renounce those that are denationalized already, and let us remain with one language, the language that was not borrowed from the foreigner, but was constructed by our race and was formed through ages together with the formation of our Lithuanian nation. The language is the life of our nation; in it is preserved the living spirit of our forefathers. We cannot, we should not, accept any Polish or White Russian language as our national language. We should remember that by introducing a few languages in a given territory we greatly burden the people in their educational work and in their affairs with the government. Not long ago, when Russia was agitated by the question of Poland's autonomy, the Poles demanded that the government of Souvalki should belong to their autonomous territory, and that the Polish language should be used in common with Russian in this territory of the Lithuanian language, so that each Lithuanian citizen would have been obliged to know three languages, Lithuanian, Polish, and Russian; otherwise, he would have been left actually without rights, and could not have taken part even in his township affairs. Is it reasonable to demand of the peasants a knowledge of so many languages, that in other countries is not demanded of even the well-educated people? Is it necessary to impose such a nonsensical burden on those people in order to satisfy the fantastic dreams of Polish politicians?

Such is our attitude toward foreign languages and relations to our neighbors. Neither with Poles nor with Russians should we have any political ties. The Lithuanian nation has already been bound to both of them by such ties for several hundreds of years. Let that suffice.

We have no special economic interest in Poland. Ours is an agricultural country, Poland is the same. Our exports we shall market better in other countries of western Europe. Up to now we received our imports mainly through Riga and Moscow. It would be more wholesome for Lithuania if the cultural ties with Poland were broken altogether. United with Poles, we should fear undesirable influences and the weakening of our independence. It is clear, then, that the uniting of Poland and Lithuania is not to the interest of Lithuanians. We have spoken before about receiving White Russians into the Lithuanian state. The Poles and Russians are foreigners to us; let each of us therefore live by ourselves, and if there is a need for economic relations they could be arranged according to the practices of other neighboring, sovereign and independent states.

On the other hand, our relations with the Letts should be closer. If Lithuania and Lett-

PRESENT NATIONAL ASPIRATIONS

land both become states, then a union of both these states would be mutually advantageous. Lithuanians and Letts are people of the same race, even their names are of the same linguistic origin. Our languages even now are so closely akin to one another that they differ no more than various German dialects of the south and north. The only difference is that history has united the German dialects of north and south, and divided the Lithuanian and Lettish. True, history has made us different nations; we could not be fully united, for then each one would wish to have the upper hand, and we should mutually injure ourselves. But we could live together in two states, united on equal terms, each one attending to its internal affairs, and in external affairs both acting together, each exerting on the other a useful national influence. In our economic affairs we would agree. We occupy contiguous territory, the Letts holding the seacoast. In a union with the Letts we would reap the benefit of the sea trade, and their seaports would have a larger hinterland. If both nations were independent of foreigners and united more closely, the mutual cultural influence would strengthen them against foreign encroachment, would purify and strengthen the Lithuanian-Lettish spirit, and also the language of both. The national traditions forgotten by the one or the other would revive by mutual influence. We are the only two sister-nations in the world, and neither one is populous.

CHAPTER VIII

IS LITHUANIA, AS A STATE, POSSIBLE? ABILITY OF LITHUANIANS FOR STATESMANSHIP; THE RIGHT TO INDEPENDENCE OF NATIONS WHICH HAVE LOST OR HAVE NEVER HAD THEIR OWN GOVERNMENT; THE FATE OF SMALL NATIONS IN FOREIGN STATES (VIZ., RUSSIA); HAVE THE LITHUANIANS A SUFFICIENT NUMBER OF EDUCATED MEN TO CONDUCT THE GOVERNMENT OF STATE? AREA AND POPULATION OF LITHUANIA COMPARED WITH THE DIFFERENT INDEPENDENT EUROPEAN STATES

IS Lithuania as a state possible?

That the Lithuanian nation can organize a state and direct it is amply demonstrated by its history. The Lithuanian nation in this has shown greater abilities than many other European nations. With the exception of the Franks it is the only example in Europe of a comparatively small nation organizing itself into a state and taking under its dominion nations many times larger than itself. And in its many conquests it is not submerged after mixture with those conquered nations, as happened in the case of the Franks. Lithuania has established her government over others and has composed a code of laws (Lithuanian Statute, 1529) when other European nations with older states than hers were making only feeble attempts in this direction. The Lithuanian statute is not the amateur creation of an individual, such as Sachsenspiegel (about 1230 A. D.), but an authoritative code of laws published by a state.

It was said by an American daily paper that the Lithuanians, who had not formed a state of their own for over five hundred years and were only a part of Poland, now desired to become a state. The implication is that the Lithuanians, who lost their statehood so long ago, should not even now possess it and that the most appropriate place for Lithuanians would be within the borders of a Polish kingdom. Every one can see in whose interest such ideas are spread. Five hundred years ago in Lithuania Vitautas was reigning, and he was the most powerful monarch in all eastern Europe. But here, perhaps, one remembers the disposition made by Jagela in Krevo. If history is understood in such a way then there is no

LITHUANIA AS A STATE

use in argument. I have demonstrated that Lithuania was a sovereign state until 1795 and only after the union of Lublin (1560) had she a real union with Poland.

If we deny the rights of a nation to be also a state on such grounds, then Norway in 1905, without the least right, had desired to be independent, and separated from Sweden. From the union of Colmar (in 1397) Norway was, without an interval, in union with Denmark. The Norwegian nation has acquired the Danish language, has forgotten its own Norwegian language; and it is only one hundred years since Sweden took Norway from Denmark by war in January, 1814. According to the author of the opinion quoted about Lithuania, Norway, if she does not wish to be with Sweden, should be returned to Denmark. Finally, the Norwegian nation is not numerous. On the declaration of its independence it had in its territory 2,240,000 inhabitants (according to statistics of 1900), and these same people did not know Norwegian, but were using the Danish language, just as some Lithuanians now speak Polish in Lithuania. And yet Norway is now independent.

Hungary and Bohemia, when the rights of succession to the throne of both states rested with Archduke Ferdinand, brother of Emperor Charles V, entered into union in 1526 and have remained in such a relation to Austria, as Lithuania had to Poland, up to our times. Only in 1867 did Austria grant to Hungary the present satisfactory constitution. After the collapse of the Bohemian uprising at the White Mountain, near Praga, in 1620, Bohemian independence was altogether destroyed and the Bohemian nation was the slave of Austria until now. The Allied states, however, warring on the Central Powers, recognize the just Bohemian aspirations; they recognize the necessity of freeing the Slovaks, who never have formed an independent state, but belonged for over one thousand years to Hungary. Not long ago Slovak Louis Kossuth was the great patriot of Hungary.

Serbians, Bulgarians, Roumanians, Greeks have been under the severest oppression since the victorious migrations of the Turks to Europe after the fall of Adrianople (1365), Kosovo battle (1389), and the capture of Constantinople (1453); only in 1829 some of them, and only in a small part of territory inhabited by them, gained their partial independence. The Congress of Berlin (1878) pushed slightly forward the work of liberating and uniting these nations. Even now, Serbia, Bosnia, Herzegovina, and Croatia may not have the right to unite for the sole reason that for many centuries they were exploited and oppressed by others, although all these provinces are parts of a single Serbo-Croatian nation. The Roumanians of Transylvania and Bessarabia are the same as the inhabitants of Moldavia and Wallachia; why should not they, being all Roumanians, possess the right to unite and govern themselves?

The peoples of Italy had been disunited since the fall of Rome. What right had the Italian patriots in 1860–1870 to abolish all the small states existing up to that time in Italy and to form from them one Italy that had no existence before, and to unite therein Italian peoples, which until then had been always divided into small dukedoms and little republics, or ruled by foreign conquerors?

All agree that the Finnish nation should be independent, although Finland never was a separate state. One hundred years ago Russia, by war, took her from Sweden and granted her autonomy; before that Finland was only part of Sweden.

If the Lithuanian nation should belong to the Polish state for the reason that one hundred years ago Lithuania was in union with Poland, so much more should Poland belong to the Russian state, because during the entire last century she was part of Russia. But all agree that the Polish nation has a right to form its own independent state; then why should the Polish politicians menace the freedom of other nations? The Lithuanian nation has the same rights to the union of all its parts and to independence as have all the other nations cited. To Lithuanian demands for independence the bureaucrats of Imperial Russia rejoined that in that case it would be necessary to grant independence to the Samoyeds. In other words, there are in Russia larger and smaller nations not of Russian extraction, and the Russian state would suffer by returning to them or granting them their former independence. To this we answer, that there is no use in speaking about the independence of Samoyeds, Chukchi, and Kamchadales who live in Siberia on the shores of Behring Sea, so long as these people themselves do not propose it and are not conscious of having certain objects, to satisfy which they would need independence. We appreciate the difficulty of the Russian statesmen in the solving the riddle of foreign nationalities in such a way that they shall not injure those nations or the Russian nation. Independence will not be needed by all the foreign nations of Russia, especially those that are very small and hold a difficult geographical position; for such, autonomy will suffice, or even more or less home rule. But we cannot refrain from demanding that which belongs to us and which is practicable; to do otherwise would be to sin against justice; being injured by others we should injure ourselves.

Some Pan-Germans, answering the Lithuanian demands for independence, called Lithuanians "Bauervolk," the peasant nation, implying that they had too few intelligent men, skilful in administrative work, to direct the state. Our answer is: The Bulgarians and Serbians on the formation of their states were a peasant people, and had fewer educated men than the Lithuanians now possess. Let us take, for example, the Bulgarians; from 1878, the year of the Congress of Berlin, until 1912, thirty-four years, they have become a complete nation, and only lately they conquered their former lords, the Turks! The Bulgarian educated classes and their statesmen are not inferior to the corresponding classes of Turkey. Without independence, would the Bulgarians, under the Turkish rule, have progressed so much? Armenia was doomed to remain under Turkey, after the Berlin Congress. Could she be compared now to Bulgaria? True, the Germans have not found many educated Lithuanians in the conquered territory of Lithuania lately, but we should remember the circumstances. Before the war there were a considerable number of educated Lithuanians in Lithuania, but they were mostly of the younger generation, under obligation to serve in the Russian army. True, there were not too many Lithuanians experienced in the administrative branch of government, and those few who were in the heart of Russia, because until the first revolution (1905) Lithuanians absolutely were not admitted to any government position in their own country, Lithuania. At the beginning of the war all the younger generation were drafted into the army. In the Russian army there were numerous officers, doctors, and other well-educated Lithuanians. Upon the occupation of Lithuania by the German army, the Russian Government had ordered evacuation not only by the regular governmental officials but by the officials of counties, districts, private schools, banks, factories, and indeed by all inhabitants. The German army of occupation has found only those in Lithuania who could not be brought to leave their country except by force, and whom the Russian army had no time to drive out. If there were some educated Lithuanians in the governmental positions or private institutions, they had to move upon the transfer of said institutions to Russia; otherwise they would have been left without the means of living. Notwithstanding the present lack of educated Lithuanians now in Lithuania, Lithuanians have their educated classes in Europe as well as in America; they have a number of officials experienced in the administration in Russia or in Lithuania, even officers of the army;

they have educated men working in the educational spheres and in manufacture. In the period of greater freedom, since 1905, Lithuanians organized and were conducting their private institutions of learning, their factories, their trade, and their credit institutions. After the war, when the Lithuanian nation is allowed to organize as an independent state, all the educated classes of that nation will return to Lithuania. Even now, during a state of war when the future of Lithuania is uncertain, educated Lithuanians in Russia are organizing for the return to their Motherland. To that end all the energies of educated Lithuanians in America will also be turned. Their present state of mind indicates that numerous educated Lithuanians of America will return to Lithuania even at risk of great loss in order to help their Motherland in her first steps toward independence. We acknowledge that such doubts about Lithuania have arisen in the minds of certain statesmen without ill-will toward Lithuanians; but we must not forget that the hidden desire of the stronger nations to hold the weaker ones in subjection though the latter would possess their national self-consciousness and desire to be independent, is not without influence, and very often suggests objections against the freedom of the weaker nations. It is hard for a man, a member of a self-conscious but subjected nation, to witness the degradation and the injuries of his nation; but it is also difficult for a member of a great and powerful nation, especially for an individual directing the affairs of one, to understand the needs of the weaker nations. Seeing their nation powerful and exalted, it is natural for them scornfully to regard those that are weak and always humiliated, as not worthy of anything better. They forget that all men have the same nature; that in all nations there are bad and good traits, and that the power of the great nations depends mainly on the extent of their population. Even among nations there are Diveses who feast sumptuously, and there are famished Lazaruses; but it is difficult to find Samaritans to extend their helping hands to the wounded nations; nearly every stronger nation, able to harm a weaker nation, yields to the temptation to do so. But democracy in all the phases of human life, even in the policies of states and in the affairs of nations, always progresses and expands. The slogan of the present war was the overthrow of the arrogant conquerors. Great honor is due the statesman who said that liberty should be returned even to those that were conquered, because "no people must be forced under sovereignty under which it does not wish to live."* Surely, the time must come when the slavery of nations will be abolished as humanity in its progress arrived at the abolition of individual slavery.

As to the territory of Lithuania, her area and the number of inhabitants are not at all too small for the formation of a state. I will quote the statistics for both from The Statesman's Year-Book of 1914. The area is computed in the English square mile. Within the boundaries of Lithuania is the whole government of Kovno, two-thirds of the government of Vilna, not all the government of Souvalki, but as much is included from the Grodno Government as is left out of Souvalki Government. Therefore, we shall compute all the Souvalki Government and shall not count the Grodno Govern-

*President Wilson's notable communication to the Russian people, June, 1917.

LITHUANIA AS A STATE

ment. The area under Prussian rule is nearly half as large as the Souvalki Government.

	Area Square Miles	Population	Population per Square Mile
Kovno Government	15,518	1,819,000	116
Two-thirds Vilna	10,787	1,326,600	121
Souvalki and part Grodno Governments	4,750	693,000	143
Prussian-Lithuania	2,375	300,000	
Whole Lithuania about	33,430	4,138,600	125 average

Now we quote the area and inhabitants of the Lettland:

	Area Square Miles	Population	Population per Square Mile
Courland Government	10,435	758,800	72
One-half Livonia Government	8,787	740,000	84
One-third Vitebsk Government	5,661	625,000	109
Whole Lettland	24,883	2,123,800	85 average

Let us now compare the statistics of smaller European states, excluding the seven largest states. I do not speak of San Marino, Andora,

Monaco, Lichtenstein; those are anomalies: their people do not form a separate nation and have no other raison d'être; they are curiosities of history. Nor should I mention the smaller duchies in the German Empire having hundreds of square miles and a few hundred thousand inhabitants. These are merely administrative parts of Germany, and their Dukes are the heads of counties with the right of succession. But let us take the states whose populations have the significance of a nation.

Greece before the war of 1912-1913 had an area of 25,000 square miles and a population of 2,700,000. In 1881, even with the recently acquired Thessaly, there were only 1,974,000 inhabitants.

Serbia before the war of 1912-1913 had an area of 18,650 square miles and a population of 2,912,000, of whom 163,000 were not Serbians. Only after the last war did Serbia equal Lithuania, with an area of 33,890 square miles and 4,548,000 inhabitants.

Bulgaria before the war of 1912-1913 had an area of 33,647 square miles with 4,337,000 inhabitants—an area and population almost equal to Lithuania.

LITHUANIA AS A STATE

Denmark has an area of 13,580 square miles (including the territory of Faroe Islands, north of England, 540 square miles) and a population of 2,775,000.

Norway has an area of 124,445 square miles and 2,392,000 inhabitants; Holland an area of 12,650 square miles and 6,000,000 inhabitants; in 1829 there were only 2,613,000 inhabitants.

Belgium has an area of 11,373 square miles and 7,400,000 inhabitants; Switzerland an area of 15,976 square miles and 3,781,000 inhabitants, of whom 565,000 are foreign residents.

Portugal has an area of 34,254 square miles; Bavaria an area of 29,290 square miles and 6,890,000 inhabitants; and newly created Albania has an area of about 11,000 square miles, with about 800,000 inhabitants.

But if Lithuania should form a federation with Lettland then there would be a large and respectable state; Lithuania with 33,430 square miles, 4,138,000 inhabitants, Lettland with 24,880 square miles, 2,123,000 inhabitants; both together, 58,300 square miles, 6,260,000 inhabitants.

Sweden has a population of 5,600,000.

Roumania covers 50,720 square miles and

has a population of 7,000,000. In 1899 she had only 5,956,000 inhabitants.

Lithuania's geographical position, especially if she is federated with Lettland, could be envied by many nations. One has only to look at the map of Europe. The territory of Lithuania-Lettland is in the very centre of Europe on the way of the best communication by sea between eastern Europe (Russia) and all the western world; the navigable rivers of Niemen and Dvina flow through all this territory; her ports are Memel, Libau, Vindau, Riga. Would it not be better if Lithuania, possessing the largest autonomy, should remain united with one of her neighboring large states, for instance Russia? Such a question is most injudicious. No nation voluntarily goes under foreign rule. If Lithuania's independence is possible, then only a fool or a traitor would vote against her independence. The nations are wronged and eliminated not in their independence, but in their subjection to other nations. If Lithuania has any commercial or other affairs in Russia or Germany then these affairs could be safeguarded better by international treaties, Lithuania being independent from both of them rather than a slave of either of them. The ideal of the future of the Lithuanians is a complete, united Lithuania, a free Lithuania; if possible, in confederation with the equally independent and undivided Lettland.

APPENDIX

AMERICAN SYMPATHY FOR THE LITHUANIANS

The American Relief Fund for Lithuanian War Sufferers, under its principal patron, late Cardinal Farley of New York, collecting funds for war sufferers, petitioned President Wilson to aid the Lithuanian war sufferers. A delegation of this fund, with the aid of General Collins, of Elizabeth, N. J., had an audience with the President early in June asking him to proclaim by executive order the day on which funds were to be collected for the Lithuanian war sufferers. President Wilson, at this audience as well as in his letter to the fund's secretary, expressed his sympathy for the Lithuanians but stated that without the resolution of Congress he could not do this.

The American Relief Fund for Lithuanian War Sufferers arranged for a series of mass-meetings in and around New York. This was done in Pennsylvania by the Lithuanians with the aid of Congressman Casey. The purpose being to bring the misery of Lithuania to the notice of Congress, which soon thereafter passed a resolution empowering the President to proclaim a Lithuanian day for November 1, 1916.

A Central Committee for the Relief of the Lithuanian War Sufferers was organized to collect funds on this day. The sum of $200,000 was collected.

LITHUANIANS INVOKE THE AID OF PRESIDENT WILSON

BROOKLYN, N. Y., June 6th, 1916.
The following resolution was drawn up by Alderman Gaynor, of New York City, N. Y., and was presented by him and adopted at a mass-meeting of the American Relief Fund for Lithuanian War Sufferers, duly called and held at Brooklyn, N. Y., Monday, June 6th, 1916.

WHEREAS, In the great conflict between the nations of Europe, our Fatherland has been devastated and its inhabitants oppressed and large numbers slain as innocent sufferers of the war; and, WHEREAS, The United States of America, being the greatest of the neutral powers of the world, wields a mighty influence with the combatant forces;

Now, THEREFORE, WE, the Rev. A. M. Milukas and the Rev. M. Pankauskas, duly authorized delegates of the American Relief Fund for Lithuanian War Sufferers, having migrated from our native land of Lithuania to this land of freedom and independence, and ever pledging our loyalty to this, our adopted country, sincerely believing and protecting the principles of America, being nevertheless in sympathy with our unfortunate brothers in the Fatherland, in the name of our people earnestly pray and implore His Excellency, Woodrow Wilson, President of the United States of America, and the members of his official family, to use their best efforts, powers, and

My dear Mr. Milukas:

I looked up the matter you mentioned to me about the issuance of proclamations for Polish and Jewish relief from my office and fi that such proclamations were issued, as you stated, but both in pursuance of special resolutions by the Senate requesting that I set a day aside for those purposes. I have in no case felt at liberty to issue such a proclamation on my own initiative; that is the reason that my recollection in that matter was so cle

I am none the less sincerely sorry that I cannot comply with a request to which m heart accedes.

Cordially and sincerely yours,

Woodrow

Rev. A. M. Milukas, Secretary,
American Relief Fund
    For Lithuanian War Sufferers,
Maspeth, Long Island, New York.

influence to bring about an ending of this great war, or at least to alleviate the suffering and to safeguard the rights, homes, and lives of oppressed Lithuania by diplomatic negotiations, as in their wise discretion may seem best;

AND BE IT FURTHER RESOLVED, That a copy of this resolution, engrossed and authenticated by the President and Secretary of the American Relief Fund for Lithuanian War Sufferers, be forwarded to His Excellency, the President of the United States of America, and he be asked to set a day apart for the contributions of our people and the friends of our undying race, the Lithuanians, to aid them to survive this great conflict.

Attest: REV. B. ZINDŽIUS, *President.*
A. M. MILUKAS, *Secretary.*

THE AMERICAN RELIEF FUND FOR LITHUANIAN WAR SUFFERERS PLEADING FOR LITHUANIA

RESOLUTIONS PETITIONING BOTH HOUSES OF CONGRESS TO EXPRESS SYMPATHY FOR LITHUANIA, IRELAND, UKRAINIA, BOHEMIA, POLAND, ETC.

During the months of June and July of 1916 the American Relief Fund for Lithuanian War Sufferers arranged for a series of mass-meetings in the States of New York, New Jersey, Connecticut, and Pennsylvania: in Waterbury, Bridgeport, New Haven, Brooklyn, New York, Elizabeth, etc. We wish to call especial attention to the first of these meetings—at Newark, N. J.

On June 17, 1916, the mass-meeting at Newark,

APPENDIX

N. J., was addressed by Major-General F. J. Collins, of Elizabeth, N. J.; City Solicitor M. Fraser, and Rev. A. Milukas, secretary of the American Relief Fund for Lithuanian War Sufferers, the latter presiding. More than five thousand Lithuanians unanimously adopted the resolutions of the American Relief Fund.

These mass-meetings were addressed by the officers of the American Relief Fund for Lithuanian War Sufferers (Revs. A. Kodis, J. Shestokas, A. Milukas, M. Pankauskas).

The following resolutions were unanimously adopted:

WHEREAS, In the great conflict between the nations of Europe, our Fatherland has been devastated and its inhabitants oppressed and large numbers slain as innocent sufferers of the war; and

WHEREAS, The United States of America, being the greatest of the neutral Powers of the world, wields a mighty influence with the combatant forces;

Now, therefore, we, the Lithuanians of Waterbury,* Conn., gathered at the mass-meeting under the auspices of the American Relief Fund for the Lithuanian War Sufferers, having migrated from our native land, Lithuania, to this land of freedom and independence, and ever pledging our loyalty to this, our adopted country, sincerely believing and living up to the principles of America, being nevertheless in sympathy with our unfortunate brethren in the Fatherland, in the name of our people earnestly pray and implore our State's representatives in both

* Or Bayonne, Bridgeport, New Philadelphia, New York, Brooklyn, Long Island City, Newark, New Haven.

Houses of Congress to use their best efforts, powers, and influence to bring about an ending to this great war, and to alleviate the suffering and to safeguard the rights, homes, and lives of the oppressed Lithuania by diplomatic negotiations, as in their wise providence may deem best.

AND BE IT FURTHER RESOLVED, That a copy of this resolution, engrossed and authenticated by the officers of the American Relief Fund for Lithuanian War Sufferers (Rev. B. Zindzius, president; Rev. M. Pankauskas, vice-president; Rev. A. Kodis, financial secretary; Rev. J. Shestokas, treasurer; and Rev. A. M. Milukas, secretary); also Messrs. Frank Luza and Anthony Karpaviczus,* be forwarded to the Representatives from our State in both Houses of Congress of the United States of America, and they be asked to pass a resolution setting apart a day for contributions to our suffering brethren, and that American diplomatic agents be directed to use their best efforts at the Peace Conference for the restoration of independence to Lithuania, as well as to other oppressed nations, as Ireland, Ukrainia, Bohemia, Poland, etc.

CONGRESSIONAL RECORD

HOUSE OF REPRESENTATIVES

Friday, July 21, 1916, pp. 13191, 13192

Aid for Lithuanians

Mr. Flood. Mr. Speaker, I ask unanimous consent to take affairs to designate a day on which the people of this country may express their sympathy

* In other localities other names were substituted.

by contributing toward the relief of the Lithuanians in the war zone.

The Speaker. The gentleman from Virginia asks unanimous consent to take up House Resolution 258 to designate a day for taking up collections for the Lithuanians in the war zone. Is there objection?

Mr. Mann. Let us have the resolution reported.

The clerk read as follows:

House Resolution 258

WHEREAS, In the various countries now engaged in war there are four millions of Lithuanians, the great majority of whom are destitute of food, shelter, and clothing; and

WHEREAS, Millions of them have been driven from their homes without warning, deprived of an opportunity to make provision for their most elementary wants, causing starvation, disease, and untold suffering; and

WHEREAS, The people of the United States of America have learned with sorrow of this plight of millions of human beings and have most generously responded to the cry for help wherever such an opportunity has reached them;

Therefore be it resolved, That in view of the misery, wretchedness, and hardships which these four millions of Lithuanians are suffering the President of the United States be respectfully asked to designate a day on which the citizens of this country may give expression to their sympathy by contributing to the funds now being raised for the relief of the Lithuanians in the war zone.

The Speaker. Is there objection?

Mr. Mann. Reserving the right to object, I

APPENDIX

would like to inquire whether the Committee on Foreign Affairs proposes also to report a resolution into the House in reference to the American citizens whose property has been destroyed and many of whose families have lost a member, all having been driven out of Mexico—whether we are going to do anything for our own citizens driven out of Mexico while we are doing something for foreign citizens.

Mr. Flood. When the time arrives the Committee on Foreign Affairs will report a resolution to take care of American citizens who have been in Mexico and whose rights of property and person have been invaded.

Mr. Mann. American citizens who have been driven out of Mexico and starving to death.

Mr. Flood. None of them are starving.

Mr. Mann. Oh, yes; many of them have nothing to live on except charity.

Mr. Flood. The government has provided money to bring them out, all who are in there; and my information is that those who are staying there are getting along comfortably.

Mr. Mann. We have appropriated money to bring them out, brought them up to the border, and dumped them down, and there they are. Their property has been lost and they have nothing to live on; while we very properly are donating money for the Lithuanians abroad, we are doing nothing for our own people.

Mr. Flood. Our people are being taken care of. If the gentleman desires to introduce a resolution and have it referred to the Committee on Foreign Affairs I assure him that the committee will promptly consider it.

Mr. Cannon. What does the gentleman mean by saying that they are being taken care of?

Mr. Flood. I do not think any of them are suffering.

Mr. Cannon. Oh, in the hearing before the Committee on Appropriations to consider a bill to pay the expenses of bringing American citizens out, it appeared that nothing is added by way of subsistence. They are released, substantially, when they get into American territory and dumped upon the charity of the communities where they are brought.

Mr. Flood. Does the gentleman know of any American citizens brought out of Mexico who are now suffering for something to eat?

Mr. Cannon. Oh, the evidence showed that they came out without property and that all the government is doing is to get them out. I do not know their names.

Mr. Flood. No; and they are not suffering. They are taken care of just as indigent people in this country are taken care of, and this resolution does not propose that the government shall take care of the Lithuanians. It simply proposes to allow charitable Americans who feel so disposed to make contributions to a fund and to relieve their suffering.

Mr. Cannon. I am in no sense opposing the gentleman's resolution. I have no doubt that the gentleman has Lithuanians in his district.

Mr. Flood. Not a single one.

Mr. Cannon. Well, there are a great many in my district, and a great many throughout the North. But there are many French people, there are many Irish, there are many Belgians, there are many English, though not so many, and there are many Austrians and Hungarians, and why does not the gentleman bring in a resolution suggesting to the good people of America that wherever there is suffering in the war zone on the other side of the water they have the liberty to, and it is suggested that they do, contribute to relieve that suffering, because evidently from the standpoint of humanity and Christianity and charity there is as much need for the relief and suffering among those people where they are fighting in concord or where they are fighting each other. I shall not object to the gentleman's resolution, but I suggest there are a hundred million people in this country, and it might be well to appeal to their charity, that all of the suffering in the war zone may be relieved.

Mr. Flood. The committee that reported this resolution will be glad to consider any such resolution that the gentleman suggests.

Mr. Britten. Mr. Chairman, will the gentleman yield?

Mr. Flood. Yes.

Mr. Britten. Did I understand the gentleman to say in reply to my colleague from Illinois (Mr. Mann) that the Americans still living in Mexico are living there comfortably?

Mr. Flood. Yes.

Mr. Britten. What information has the gentleman or his committee that Americans living in Mexico are living there comfortably to-day?

Mr. Flood. I have information that comes from the State Department that there are no Americans who are suffering.

Mr. Britten. Then, why did we appropriate $300,000 to bring them out, if they are living there comfortably?

Mr. Flood. Mr. Speaker, we appropriated the money so that in case there was any trouble there which would endanger their lives, they might escape it.

Mr. Britten. The gentleman says that they are living in a comfortable condition in Mexico, and yet we appropriate $300,000 to improve those conditions by taking them away from there.

Mr. Flood. And some of them are living in comfortable conditions here in this country.

Mr. Britten. Are we making their conditions more comfortable in this country than in Mexico?

Mr. Flood. I do not know about that. At the present time those in Mexico may be more comfortable than those here, but at the time the appropriation was made it was necessary to bring them out of Mexico.

Mr. Britten. Why?

Mr. Flood. I stated why to the gentleman, and if he desires to object to the resolution, let him object to it, but I am not going to reply to any more silly questions.

Mr. Britten. The silliness all comes from that side of the House.

Mr. Ferris. Mr. Speaker, I demand the regular order.

The Speaker. The regular order is demanded.

Mr. Stafford. Mr. Chairman, I would like to inquire of the gentleman about the character of the resolution. The resolution we passed the other day providing for a national tag day for the benefit of the Americans was a concurrent resolution?

Mr. Flood. It was.

Mr. Stafford. Why did not the gentleman in this instance adopt the policy that these resolutions calling upon the President to name a tag day should be concurrent rather than a mere House resolution, as this is?

Mr. Flood. Mr. Speaker, the gentleman will recall that there was a Senate resolution, not a concurrent resolution, in reference to the Syrians and the Jews and the Poles and a concurrent resolution in reference to the Americans. The gentleman from Pennsylvania (Mr. Casey), who introduced this resolution, simply introduced the House resolution, and the President having issued proclamations on Senate resolutions therefore the committee thought he could just as readily issue his proclamation on a House resolution, and reported the House resolution instead of a concurrent resolution.

Mr. Stafford. Does not the gentleman think that in these matters both bodies should approve the calling upon the President to name a day for a tag for such a purpose?

Mr. Flood. I think not. A concurrent resolution may give more dignity, though I do not think it makes any difference.

The Speaker. Is there objection?

Mr. Buchanan (of Illinois). Mr. Speaker, reserving the right to object—

Mr. Ferris. Mr. Speaker, I demand the regular order.

The Speaker. The regular order is demanded.

Mr. Buchanan (of Illinois). I do not desire to object, but I am seeking information, the same as others.

The Speaker. But the Chair is bound to pursue the rules of the House.

Mr. Buchanan (of Illinois). I would like to ask who controls the territory in which these people are?

The Speaker. Is there objection. (After a pause.) The Chair hears none. The question is on agreeing to the resolution.

The resolution was agreed to.

APPENDIX

PROCLAMATION OF THE PRESIDENT

WHEREAS, I have received from the House of Representatives of the United States a resolution, passed July 21, 1916, reading as follows:

WHEREAS, In the various countries now engaged in war there are four millions of Lithuanians, the greater majority of whom are destitute of food, shelter, clothing, and

WHEREAS, Millions of them have been driven from their homes without warning, deprived of an opportunity to make provisions for their most elementary wants, causing starvation, disease, and untold suffering; and

WHEREAS, The people of the United States of America have learned with sorrow of this plight of millions of human beings, and have most generously responded to the cry of help whenever such an opportunity has reached them;

Therefore be it resolved, That in view of the misery, wretchedness, and hardships which these four millions of Lithuanians are suffering the President of the United States be respectfully asked to designate a day on which the citizens of this country may give expression to their sympathy by contributing to the funds now being raised for the relief of the Lithuanians in the war zone.

And whereas, I feel confident that the people of the United States will be moved to aid a people stricken by war famine, and disease;

Now, therefore, I, Woodrow Wilson, President of the United States, in compliance with the request of the House of Representatives thereof, do appoint and proclaim Wednesday, November 1, 1916, as a day upon which the people of the United States may make contributions as they feel disposed for the aid of the stricken Lithuanian people.

Contributions may be addressed to the American Red Cross, Washington, D. C., which will care for proper distribution.

In witness whereof, I have hereunto set my hand and caused the seal of the United States to be affixed.

Done at the City of Washington, this thirty-first day of August, in the year of our Lord one thousand nine hundred and sixteen, and of the Independence of the United States the one hundred and forty-first.

(Signed) WOODROW WILSON.

APPENDIX

APOSTOLIC DELEGATION
United States of America

1811 Biltmore Street,
Washington, D. C., October 8, 1917.

No. 4348-e.
This No. should be prefixed to the answer.

Rev. Fathers B. Zindžius, J. Shestokas, and A. Kodis,
> *Of the American Relief Fund for Lithuanian War Sufferers.*

Reverend dear Fathers.

I sent your check of 30,000 Lire to the Holy Father through His Eminence, Cardinal Gasparri, Secretary of State to His Holiness, and asked him to take charge of its being dispensed for the relief of the Catholic Lithuanians who inhabit the territory which was occupied or is occupied by belligerent armies.

In answer I have received a letter from His Eminence, the Cardinal Secretary of State, who informs me that he has transmitted the sum in question to the Executive of the Lithuanian Committee of Lausanne, Switzerland, to be distributed in favor of the Lithuanian war sufferers.

His Eminence also asks me to tell you that His Holiness was very much pleased by your devotion, and that he encourages you to continue the good work which you are doing, and that he sends you his Apostolic blessing.

With the kind regards and best wishes, I beg to remain, Reverend Fathers,

Sincerely yours in Christ,
(Signed) JOHN BONZANO,
Archbishop of Melitene, Apostolic Delegate.

(Extract from the article in Free Lithuania, describing the activities of American Relief Fund for Lithuanian War Sufferers.)

AMERICAN LITHUANIANS' PETITION TO HIS HOLINESS POPE BENEDICT XV

We, the Roman Catholic Lithuanians, kneeling at the throne of His Holiness, wish to express our filial devotion to the Apostolic See and our gratitude for all the favors that His Holiness has shown toward the Lithuanian nation.

Your Holiness! It is the great misery of our beloved brothers in Lithuania that has forced us to approach your tender heart. Since the outbreak of the European conflict our country has been the arena of many struggles between the Russian and German armies, and has become almost entirely devastated. Our fathers and brothers are forcibly enrolled in the two opposing belligerent armies, while destitute aged people, women, and children have no shelter and are enduring untold sufferings of hunger and cold, many of them prematurely having already gone to their graves. It is especially hard for the little ones who, on account of lack of the proper food, cannot withstand the hardships of the war.

Although the sufferings of Lithuania are much greater than those of Belgium and Poland because the two great armies several times have crossed and recrossed the Lithuanian plains, destroying and confiscating everything on their way, nevertheless the charitable hand of the world, while helping others, as Belgium, Poland, etc., has not been extended to Lithuania. Many individuals of different nationalities have contributed for the suffering Lithuanians, but as those donations were transmitted through the Polish Committee in Vilna, they did not reach the Lithuanian sufferers, the money being used for the establishment of Polish schools in Lithuania for the purpose of Polonizing our nation.

It is a sad fact that Lithuania has been lately so little known to the world that even the name of Lithuania has been erased from the map of Europe, and not having representatives either at the courts of the Great Powers or with the Apostolic See there has been no way by which Lithuanian rights could be defended, nor the misfortunes of that country told to the world.

From the very beginning of the war we have organized relief committees among our own people, but on account of the great army of destitutes we are lacking power and means to bring the necessary relief to them.

Therefore, forced by the necessity and prompted by your generous heart toward suffering humanity, we most humbly ask Your Holiness to set apart a day in which the Catholic people, by generous donations in the churches, could show their charity to the starving widows and orphans of Lithuania.

We pray you, Holy Father, to bless us and our country and further extend your paternal care.

This petition was obtained at and indorsed by the convention of representatives from the Lithuanian National Council of America, Lithuanian National Fund for the War Sufferers, Lithuanian Roman Catholic Federation of America, Lithuanian Roman Catholic Total Abstinence Alliance, Lithuanian Roman Catholic Federation of Labor, Lithuanian Roman Catholic Women's Alliance of America, and Knights of Lithuania, held on January 10–11, 1917, at Pittsburgh, Pa.

It was voted that a copy of this petition, through the delegates, Rev. J. J. Jakaitis and Doctor J. J. Bielskis, be presented to the Apostolic Delegate, His Excellency Mgr. John Bonzano, of Washington, D. C., for transmission to His Holiness Pope Benedict XV.

REV. JOHN J. JAKAITIS,
President of the Lithuanian National Fund for the War Sufferers.

DR. JULIUS J. BIELSKIS,
President of the Lithuanian National Council of America.

APPENDIX

AMERICAN LITHUANIANS' DECLARATION

(HANDED TO THE PRESIDENT OF THE UNITED STATES; THE APOSTOLIC DELEGATE AND THE AMBASSADORS OF THE EUROPEAN COUNTRIES AT WASHINGTON, D. C., IN THE MONTH OF JANUARY, 1917.)

The Lithuanian nation, a separate branch of the Indo-European race, has been dwelling since prehistoric times on the southwest coast of the Baltic Sea in the basin of Niemen.

Of all nations living on the Baltic coast, Lithuania alone was a powerful state in the thirteenth century. In the fourteenth century the boundaries of the Lithuanian state reached from the Baltic Sea to the Black Sea. In times of her political strength Lithuania stopped the advance of the Teutons toward the east (1410), and by thus checking the advance of the Teutons, assisted in maintaining the equilibrium of Europe. From the other side Lithuania, with her own breast, protected Europe's Christian civilization from the onflow of the Tartar hordes.

Lithuania in such times did not know slavery. For ages she formed her own political traditions and her own independent customs. Although in the sixteenth century, on account of the wars with the Muscovites, Lithuanian noblemen were forced to form a political union with the Poles (similar to that now existing between Austria and Hungary), nevertheless, up to the partition of Poland and Lithuania (latter part of eighteenth century) not only did Lithuania maintain her national individualism, but she succeeded also in maintaining her own political self-government.

Later, on, in times of great pressure from the side of Russia, although all Lithuanian presses were closed, and no papers or books were printed in the country from 1864 to 1904, the Lithuanian desire and hope for independence was not subdued. The vision of independence was kept alive in the peasant songs and in the literature printed outside the Russian boundaries.

In the year 1905 the Lithuanian nation played a great part in the movement for the emancipation of different nationalities composing the Russian Empire. The same year (November 21 and 22) about two thousand Lithuanian delegates from all parts of Lithuania gathered in the city of Vilna, the old capitol of Lithuania. All Lithuanian political parties were represented and the delegates unanimously demanded political freedom for Lithuania.

Later, severe suppression on the part of Russia prevented the attainment of independence. Nevertheless, the Lithuanians gained the right in some degree to cultivate the field of literature and education, and during ten years of peaceful cultural work the people have shown unusual skill and adaptness in writing and in organizing schools and educational societies. Periodicals and literature in general have circulated throughout the country, educational and economic institutions have sprung up, and the people have built up their own commerce and industry.

The great European war has found Lithuania thus building itself up, while at the same time politically divided between the two powerful governments of Russia and Germany. Lithuanians have been forced in retreating to devastate their own native country, and in advancing have been compelled to waste the country of their brothers who are forced to serve in the armies of one or the other of the belligerents.

At this critical moment, when the world is called upon to solve a very important problem, namely, that of establishing a humane, and assuring a lasting peace, WE, THE EMPOWERED REPRESENTATIVES OF THE LITHUANIAN NATION, assume the privilege and duty of declaring that it is our sincere belief that lasting peace can be established only if every living nation be given the right to determine her own destiny.

IN THE NAME OF OUR NATION WE DECLARE THAT:

WHEREAS, Lithuanians, since prehistoric times have dwelt in the same place without seeking to add to their territory by any form of conquest, and

WHEREAS, Lithuania has shown great power of organization and ability to rule herself upon her own soil, and

WHEREAS, political freedom of Lithuania has become an inalienable attribute of the Lithuanian life and spirit, and

WHEREAS, Lithuania has had a glorious political part and has made signal sacrifices on behalf of humanity, and

WHEREAS, Lithuania, in the thirteenth century, was wholly united under one government, and for centuries maintained its union and independence, and

WHEREAS, united and politically independent Lithuania could accomplish her cultural and national ideals, and be of real benefit to the whole of humanity, and

WHEREAS, divided and repressed Lithuania would be a constant menace ever threatening European peace.

THEREFORE, BE IT RESOLVED: That we, the empowered representatives of the Lithuanian nation, demand of the representatives of the governments that will, at the close of the war, negotiate peace:

(1) That ethnographical Lithuania be united in one political body, and

(2) That united Lithuania be given absolute political independence, and

BE IT FURTHER RESOLVED: That the Reverend John Zilius and Doctor Julius J. Bielskis be, and they hereby are, empowered and instructed to present a copy of this declaration to the ambassadors of all European countries, and to publish this declaration in such manner as they deem to be to the best interests of the Lithuanian people.

LITHUANIAN NATIONAL COUNCIL OF AMERICA,
    By Its Component Representatives:
Lithuanian Roman Catholic Alliance of America,
    By
National Fund,
    By

APPENDIX

Lithuanian Roman Catholic Federation of America,
   By
Lithuanian Total Abstinence Alliance,
   By
Lithuanian Federation of Labor,
   By
Lithuanian Roman Catholic Women's Alliance of America,
   By
Knights of Lithuania.
   PRESIDENT, DR. JULIUS J. BIELSKIS,
      53 Capital Ave., Hartford, Conn.
   SECRETARY, DR. FR. AUGUSTAITIS,
      614 W. Mahanoy Ave., Mahanoy City, Pa.

CONVENTION OF THE LITHUANIANS OF AMERICA

March 13-14, 1918, a convention of the Lithuanians residing in the United States of America was held at the Madison Square Garden Theatre, New York City. The 1,500 delegates, representing 1,000 organizations and colonies, assembled for the purpose of declaring their determined will regarding the future of their mother country, Lithuania.

The following resolutions were adopted:

WHEREAS, The Lithuanian Nation forms an ethnographic, cultural, economic, and political inseparable body; and

WHEREAS, The historic past of Lithuania and the present democratic development of the world reaffirms to the Lithuanian Nation the undeniable right to re-establish its own sovereign State; and

WHEREAS, In the question of its ultimate political destiny the Lithuanian Nation maintains the right to follow its own national ideals; and

WHEREAS, Nations can successfully pursue their cultural courses and develop their economic resources only when in possession of their full political freedom; and

WHEREAS, Every nation has an inherent right to decide its own political destiny; and

WHEREAS, The present war conditions have rendered the recognition of Lithuanian political freedom of international importance and therefore it becomes a subject to be deliberated upon at the international peace congress; and

WHEREAS, Only the international congress can give a true guarantee of the political sovereignty of Lithuania and not any warring nation striving now to enslave Lithuania; and

WHEREAS, Our highly esteemed President, Woodrow Wilson, adheres to the principle declared by him to the United States Senate, January 22, 1917, that

"No peace can last, or ought to last, which does not recognize and accept the principle that governments derive all their just powers from consent of the governed, and that no right anywhere exists to hand people about from sovereignty to sovereignty as if they were property."

THEREFORE, the Convention of the Lithuanians of America, after grave consideration of the present political situation of Lithuania, resolved,

I.—To respectfully request the President of the United States and the allied as well as the neutral governments of the world, to recognize the following demands:

1. That for the full and unhindered development of Lithuania it is necessary that Lithuania become a sover-

eign and independent democratic state within its own ethnographic boundaries, with the necessary economic corrections.

2. That the independence of Lithuania be assured by the international peace congress, and that delegates of Lithuania be given right to take part with full deliberative powers.

II.—That these resolutions be respectfully presented to our highly esteemed President, Woodrow Wilson, who has unceasingly championed protection of the rights of small and subject nationalities, and to all allied and neutral governments.

BE IT FURTHER RESOLVED, That the President, Woodrow Wilson, and the nations of the world, be respectfully requested that the right to a separate and deliberative representation at the impending international peace conference be given to the representatives of the people of Lithuania.

LITHUANIANS PLACE THEIR HOPES OF INDEPENDENCE ON PRESIDENT WILSON AND POPE BENEDICT XV

The mass-meeting of Lithuanian residents of counties of Queens and Nassau, of the State of New York, was held on September 23, 1917, at the Parochial Hall of Transfiguration Church, Hull Avenue and Remsen Place, Maspeth, New York City.

The addresses were made by Rev. A. M. Milukas, rector of Transfiguration Church, Rev. Dr. A. Maliauskis, of Chicago, and Mr. A. Novicki, of

Maspeth. The following resolutions were unanimously adopted:

WHEREAS, The aggressions and outrages of autocracy against the liberty of the people forced the United States to take arms to defend the peoples' rights and liberty on land and sea.

WHEREAS, The United States being morally, physically, and materially one of the most powerful countries can accomplish great things in this direction.

WHEREAS, The United States entered the war with all her powers will bring the victory for democracy.

WHEREAS, During this war the small nations suffered the most and some of them are entirely devastated.

WHEREAS, Lithuania on eastern battle-front for three years serving as a battle-field and contributing half a million of her sons for the Allied armies, thereby taking an active part in the war for liberty and justice.

WHEREAS, The most appreciated words of President Wilson in the recent note to Russia and also the proclaimed principle of nationalities by the Allies assure the restoration of liberty for the small nations.

WHEREAS, We are especially grateful to President Wilson as well as His Holiness Pope Benedict XV for their efforts to restore the freedom of peoples living in the territories of the former Poland, that is the historical dual Polish-Lithuanian state, but the experience of centuries has amply proved that the union of peoples of different nationality and race, as are Lithuanians and Poles, under their dual and independent governments, could produce only a continuous strife, disorder, and anarchy, the principal cause of the final fall of both those united nations.

Therefore be it resolved, That we, the Lithuanians of

APPENDIX

the State of New York having immigrated from our native land, Lithuania, to this land of liberty, and ever pledging our loyalty to this our adopted country, sincerely believing and living up to the principles of the United States of America, being nevertheless in sympathy with our brothers in Lithuania.

(1) We appeal to the Congress of the United States through the representatives of our State, that the Congress of the United States discussing peace terms should include the demand for the restoration of Lithuania not in union with Poland, but as a separate state.

(2) That the Government of the United States support the rights of all nations participating or affected in this war, be they large or small. That these rights can only be satisfactorily adjusted after considering the just claims of the representatives of respective nations.

(3) We earnestly pray and implore the representatives of our State in both Houses of the United States Congress to bring to pass the above measure.

Be it further resolved, That Dr. J. J. Bielskis, be, and he hereby is, empowered and instructed to present a copy of this resolution to the representatives of the State of New York in both Houses of the United States Congress at Washington, D. C.

A. M. MILUKAS, *President.*

[SEAL]   A. NOVICKI, *Secretary.*

Sworn and subscribed before me this 4th day of October, 1917.

KAZIMIER BRUSAK, *Notary Public.*
Notary Public, Kings Co.; Kings Co. Reg. No. 9032; Kings Co. Clerk's No. 203.

APPENDIX

HOUSE OF REPRESENTATIVES, U. S.
COMMITTEE ON MILITARY AFFAIRS
WASHINGTON, D. C., October 10, 1917.

REV. A. M. MILUKAS.

Dear Sir: I have your copy of resolutions adopted by Lithuanians and I am heartily in sympathy with the ideas they convey. Am sorry Congress is not in session or I would have them put in the Congressional Record.

If there is any way in which I can be of service to you, I shall be glad.

Sincerely,

GEO. R. LUNN.

July 4th, 1918.

HIS EXCELLENCY PRESIDENT WOODROW WILSON,
White House, Washington, D. C.

As it behooves good American Roman Catholics of Lithuanian descent we began this day with prayers in our church for the success of our armies on the field of battle, and for the welfare of our dear boys in our country's service. Now we are to start on New York's loyalty parade, proudly carrying in front of us Old Glory, and our church service flags with 106 stars out of 500 male membership. We turn to greet you as our Chief Commander, pledging our lives and properties on the altar of our country.

We hope and pray that in the near future you, Mr. President, as the leader of victorious allies will be able to vindicate the violated democracy, to restore with our Holy Father the Pope, the right and justice, and that among other things you will help to re-establish on the shore of the Baltic Sea a free and independent Lithuanian state.

A. M. MILUKAS, *Rector*,
Alex Grabauskas } *Trustees*,
Simon Cerebejus
Of Transfiguration Church, Maspeth, L. I., New York City.

WASHINGTON, July 6, 1918.

MY DEAR SIR:

Allow me to acknowledge the receipt of your telegram of July 4th and to say that I shall have pleasure in bringing it to the attention of the President.

In his behalf let me thank you and all those concerned for your friendly and patriotic assurances.

Sincerely yours,

J. P. TUMULTY,
Secretary to the President.

Rev. A. M. Milukas,
Maspeth, Long Island, N. Y.

APPENDIX

THE RESOLUTION OF THE LITHUANIAN NATIONAL COUNCIL

We, the Lithuanian National Council, representing the central organizations, comprising about 750,000 Lithuanians of America, in a joint session held November 27th, 1918, in the Hotel McAlpin in the City of New York, have unanimously adopted the following resolution:

1. WHEREAS, Provisional Government of Lithuania has been duly elected by the State Council of Lithuania, consisting of Professor Augustinas Voldemaras as Premier and Minister of Foreign Affairs; Martinas Ychas, ex-member of Russian Duma from Lithuania, as Minister of Treasury; Doctor Alexas Alekna as Minister of the Interior; Major-General Žukauskis as Minister of War; Doctor Jokantas as Minister of Education; Engineer Stasys Liandsbergis as Minister of Communication; Count Alexander Tyškevičius as Minister of Agriculture; Judge Kriščiukaitis as Minister of Justice; Attorney Petras Leonas, ex-member of Russian Duma from Lithuania, as State Comptroller.

2. WHEREAS, The newly elected Government of Lithuania possesses confidence of the majority of the people and is able to maintain justice, to preserve peace and order in the country and to perform necessary reconstruction work until the Constitutional Assembly shall be convened at Vilnius.

3. WHEREAS, In Lithuania there has been

formed an army consisting of 60,000 men or more to enforce peace and order and to support Provisional Government.

Therefore Be It Resolved, 1. That we, representatives of the Lithuania National Council, recognize the authority of the Provisional Government and hereby pledge our fervent support to it.

2. That we respectfully request President Woodrow Wilson, the Government and the people of the United States to recognize the independence and sovereignty of the Lithuanian nation and her Provisional Government as the legal and official representative body of Lithuania.

3. That representatives of the Government of Lithuania shall be admitted to deliberations, decisions and actions at the Peace Conference.

4. That we fully believe in principles of democracy as expressed by President Woodrow Wilson and are staunch supporters of creating a League of Nations and that the Lithuanian nation shall be admitted to the membership.

5. *It is further Resolved*, That a copy of these resolutions be sent to President Woodrow Wilson, Secretary of State Robert Lansing, and Chairmen of the Foreign Relations Committee of the Senate.

J. S. LOPATTO, *Chairman*.
V. F. JANKAUSKAS, *Secretary*.

LITHUANIANS IN AMERICA PROVE THEIR PATRIOTISM TO THEIR ADOPTED COUNTRY

Treasury Department
Second Federal Reserve District
Brooklyn Liberty Loan Committee
Headquarters District 93, 102 Montague Street, Brooklyn, N. Y.

October 23, 1918.

St. George's Church,
 207 York Street, Brooklyn.
Rev. A. P. Kodis:

Beg to advise you that total subscriptions received from your church amount to $10,950 for the Fourth Liberty Loan.

Thanking you for your co-operation, we are
  Yours for the Fourth Liberty Loan,
   J. M. Heatherton,
    Chairman Precinct 93.

P. S.—Your additional subscriptions received to-day make a total amount of $41,950.

Similar letters were received by nearly a hundred of the Lithuanian Roman Catholic rectors in this country. The official figures of the Liberty Loan Committee show that Lithuanians are ahead of many more numerous nationalities of the U. S. A. in their patriotic works.

APPENDIX

LITHUANIANS AT THE INTERNATIONAL CONFERENCE

June 27-29, 1916, at the International Conference, Lausanne, Switzerland, where twenty-eight nations were represented, five accredited Lithuanian delegates were present—three from Lithuania and two from the United States of America. During a session of the conference a long Lithuanian declaration was read, which, after reciting the historical events in the Lithuanian state, presented the following conclusion:

"Relying on these bases, the Lithuanian nation with its own traditions, culture, national ideals and its individuality, believe that the only way a nation can survive is to acquire its own rights in all domains of life, and that the nation should direct its own destiny. The young Lithuania presenting the facts that for centuries Lithuania was an independent state, and now asking for her own rights, it is not her object to impose on the rights of those nations which were included and formed a part of the Grand Duchy of Lithuania.

"The Lithuanian nation, which for centuries experienced so much disappointment, sees the guarantee of her future and the sufficient guarantee of her freedom only in the complete independence of Lithuania."

Over 200,000 Lithuanian refugees in Russia who were forced to abandon their homes and flee to unknown countries, to be scattered in all parts of Russia, called a conference at Petrograd, May 27,

1917, to consider, through their delegates, the situation of their mother country, Lithuania.

The following is a conclusion of the adopted resolutions:

BE IT RESOLVED: 1. That the ethnographic Lithuania be established into an independent state, continually neutral.
2. The independence and neutrality of Lithuania must be guaranteed at the Peace Congress.
3. Lithuanian representatives must be admitted to the Peace Congress.

LITHUANIA SEPARATED FROM RUSSIA

In 1915 Germany took the whole of Lithuania from Russia, established custom-houses and fixed the boundaries between Lithuania, Germany, and Poland. The people of this country are being called citizens of Lithuania.

The only tie that bound Lithuania to Russia was the Czar, as he had the title of Grand Duke of Lithuania, but now that he is deposed, ipso facto, Lithuania becomes separated from Russia. Russia is now a republic, and the hands of Lithuania are again freed.

In the latter part of 1917 Germany transferred the reins of government in Lithuania from the German military to the Lithuanian civil government.

The Lithuanian Diet was called September 18-22, 1917, at the city of Vilna; 215 delegates, representing all parts of the country and all political parties in Lithuania, assembled to confer concerning the destiny of Lithuania. The Valstijos Taryba (State Council) composed of 20 persons, representing all political parties, was organized.

A NATION MARTYR

(Rev. Dr. A. Maliauskis, in *Philadelphia Press*, 1916.)

The fearful European War has throttled with its bloody hand the innocent, unoffending, peacefully abiding, and patiently bearing Lithuanian people under the rule of both Germany and Russia.

The idol of war, the inhuman desires of the oppressors, are threatening the Lithuanian nation with final destruction.

Because many are not familiar with the misfortunes of Lithuania we will briefly attempt to inform them.

Lithuanians are neither Slavs nor Germans, but a separate branch of an Indo-European people. The Lithuanian language is far more ancient than the Slavonian and has a pedigree of nobility strikingly resembling the archaic Sanscrit.

During the Middle Ages when Lithuania was governed by her own rulers, Mindaugas, Gediminas, Algirdas, Kestutis, Vitautas, Jagela, she was one of the most powerful nations of Europe.

Her boundaries extended from the Baltic to the

Black Sea. The Poles, her neighbors, wishing to strengthen their domain, invited Jagela, the Lithuanian ruler, to the throne of Poland (1385). From that time Lithuania and Poland had a common King.

In 1569 a confederation was formed between Poland and Lithuania. Poles, however, proved to be not pleasant companions. They took away from Lithuania the rich provinces of Podolia, Volynia, and Kiev. That stirred up an internal discord which naturally weakened the mutual power of both nations. Finally Russia, Prussia, and Austria, taking advantage of that internal strife, toward the close of the eighteenth century divided among themselves the both nations. The large portion of Lithuania was seized by Russia, the smaller by Prussia.

From that time started a long and incessant oppression, Germany striving to Germanize Lithuanians and Russia to Russianize them.

In Russia there prevails a national orthodox religion. The fact of being orthodox implies being a Russian. Russia overran Lithuania with its orthodox priests with the purpose of proselytizing Lithuania to the national orthodox religion, and thereby striving to induce them to be Russianized.

But the rude orthodox priests of Russia by their conduct incurred rather the hatred of the people than the conversion which they sought.

The Russian Government, however, attempted

APPENDIX 145

even stronger means of Russianizing Lithuanians. In 1864 she strictly prohibited the study of the Lithuanian language and abolished the Lithuanian press.

But the people, however, were anxious for education. They could not forget their lost liberty. Secretly and by stealth they brought Lithuanian literature from Prussian Lithuania and disseminated it among the people. Secretly and by night, hidden from Russian police and gendarmes, they read these books and papers and taught their children to read.

Woe befell them whom the Russian Government found teaching to their children their own language or spreading the Lithuanian literature. Upon such they imposed enormous fines, imprisoned them, or even sent them to Siberia, where they were compelled to meet death by murderous hand or ferocious beasts.

Thus suffered Lithuania for forty years. Finally the Russian Government was convinced that notwithstanding its ferocious persecutions and prohibition of literature and education almost all the Lithuanians were able to read and write in their own tongue.

At the outbreak of the revolution the Russian Government, in order to gain the Lithuanian goodwill and at the same time in order to prevent them joining the revolution, on the 10th of April, 1904, allowed the restoration of the Lithuanian press.

Lithuania suffered not less even in the economic

line. Russia, forming commercial treaties with Germany, did not consider Lithuania. Lithuania is almost exclusively an agricultural country. The sources of its wealth are almost entirely in agriculture. But, thanks to commercial treaties, Lithuania could not sell its produce in Germany nor procure from Germany necessary machinery or other implements by reason of the exorbitant tariff, so that Lithuanians were unable to sell their products for obtainable profit and were obliged to pay exorbitant prices for inferior machinery and other implements manufactured by Russia.

The union of endeavor for economic improvement was greatly discouraged and hindered by the Russian Government, and although through great pressure organization could be perfected, still they were not sure of permanent existence. Any higher official or governor has legislative, executive, and judicial power in Lithuania. This was abolished in England in the fourteenth century. Those officials can dissolve any organization according to their whim, though without any reason.

All officials throughout, from the lowest to the highest, were Russians sent from Russia, knowing neither the customs of the people nor the demands of the country, though the most learned Lithuanian could not be an official in his own country.

The conditions have not improved even during the war. The leading paper of Russia, Novoje Vremia, time and again deplores that Russia is

APPENDIX 147

weak and not able to withstand the German invasion because being composed of many nationalities, whilst Germany is one.

And, above all, that paper maintains that Russia must exert her utmost power to abolish after the war a plurality of nations and have all nations combined in one.

Of the same opinion is the strongest nationalist party. Hence while Lithuania's children are shedding their blood in defense of the Russian Power, Russia is planning a final destruction for the Lithuanians.

Germany has the same designs over Lithuania. Professor Dr. T. Kochler, in the Vossische Zeitung, No. 145, of 1916, philosophically explains how to denationalize Lithuania. The renowned German writer, Dr. P. Rohrbach, in his work Russland und Wir (Russia and We), (Stuttgart, 1915), writes that the aim of Germany is to Germanize Lithuania. To accomplish this the government is to buy the Lithuanian lands and to have them colonized by Germans. When there will be in Lithuania more Germans than Lithuanians then the denationalization will be easily accomplished. Of the same opinion is the German statesman, Broderic Kurmahlen, in his work, New Eastern Country, published in Berlin in 1915.

Thus each promises to Lithuania nothing but final destruction.

Because the great magnanimous American people have for their ideal the liberty and humanity of all nations, the martyred Lithuanian nation is supplicating for aid in the hope that the noble American people, with their authoritative word, will help Lithuania to destroy the iron bonds and throw aside the oppressing yoke of the strangers.

1,000,000 LEFT HOMES AS RUSSIANS RETIRED

LITHUANIAN PRIEST DESCRIBES HEAVY TRIALS OF GREAT ARMY OF REFUGEES

A movement to help the hundreds of thousands of Lithuanians, Letts, Poles, and Jews who were swept along with the retiring Russian armies will be undertaken here by Rev. Dr. Anthony Maliauskis, a Lithuanian priest, who reached here on Wednesday on the Norwegian steamer *Frederick VIII*. Before he left Russia he went from Vilna to Petrograd and obtained first-hand information regarding the conditions of these refugees, estimated at more than 1,000,000 men, women, and children. According to the best estimates accessible, these refugees include some 500,000 Lithuanians and 200,000 Jews. More than 160,000 families are involved in this exodus caused by the eastern war.

"A Russian general staff officer told me," said Dr. Maliauskis, "that as these great crowds of refugees were swept onward by the retiring movements of the troops many of them fell exhausted and died of hunger by the roadside. Others tried to ward off starvation by eating every green thing to be found in the fields and forests. Even the grass and shrubs by the roadside were devoured. In the stress and confusion of the time it was impossible for the military to afford any aid whatsoever, as the latter could not provide for its own needs.

"Some of the few Russian refugees found friends or relatives, it is said. But the other homeless ones, many of whom were swept forward to points as distant as Moscow and even farther, found that no provision could be made to shelter so vast a number or to feed them. A majority of them were from the Russian Lithuanian provinces of Kovno, Suvalki, and Vilna.

"I was told that thousands of women and children were living in fields and forests without food, many of them ill from privation and exposure on the long and weary flight. All are helpless, for everything they own has been wiped out. With conditions as they are at present, and the vast number of persons to be cared for, it is extremely doubtful if they can expect any aid from Russian charity in the immediate future.

"The plight of these refugees from the eastern battle-front appears to be far worse than anything of the kind that afflicted the people of Belgium. I have come over here to make an appeal direct to the Lithuanians to aid them. There are about

500,000 Lithuanians in America and 10 per cent of them are in New York. . . .

"The condition of many of the people in the Lithuanian provinces of Russia, who have been buffeted back and forth between the two great forces in two invasions and many battles, is not a great deal better than that of the refugees. In many cases their homes and property are lost, and they are without resources of any kind except the bare land."—*New York Times*, October 30, 1915.

400,000 FARMS RUINED BY FOE IN LITHUANIA

150,000 Starving and Penniless Civilians Living in Cellars and Dugouts

Geneva, May 18.—The Lithuanian Bureau at Lausanne has made public statistics received from the region of Lithuania occupied by the Germans. From these it appears that 150,000 civilians are penniless and starving, living in cellars and dugouts.

Four hundred thousand farms in that region are reported to have been devastated. The death-rate is said to be growing alarmingly on account of the unsanitary conditions under which the people are living.—*New York Times*, May 19, 1917.

CASE OF LITHUANIA FOR INDEPENDENCE

UNITED STATES SENATOR LODGE IN FAVOR OF FREE LITHUANIA

We read in the Congressional Record, vol 57, December 3, 1918:

MR. LODGE. Mr. President, I have here a statement of the committee representing the Lithuanian associations in this country. Lithuania is a country for which, I am sure, any one who has examined the facts feels deepest sympathy, which I hope will be given independent government and freedom in the terms of peace. I desire to present in their behalf to the Senate their case for independence, as they call it, and ask that it be printed as a public document and be referred to the Committee on Foreign Relations.

THE VICE-PRESIDENT. Without objection, it is so ordered.

APPENDIX

LITHUANIAN ORGANIZATIONS IN AMERICA ENGAGED IN THE WORK OF RESTORING THE INDEPENDENT STATE OF LITHUANIA

LITHUANIA NATIONAL COUNCIL, representing:
Lithuanian Roman Catholic Alliance of America, National Fund (raised over $400,000), Lithuanian Roman Catholic Federation of America, Lithuanian Total Abstinence Union, Lithuanian Federation of Labor, Lithuanian Roman Catholic Women's Alliance of America, and Knights of Lithuania.
Council on Lithuanian National Affairs.
Society of Lithuanian Patriots.
Lithuanian Labor Council.
Lithuanian Alliance of America.
Lithuanian National League.
Lithuanian Independence Fund.
Lithuanian National Fund.
Lithuanian Development Corporation.
Young Men's Circle.
Lithuanian National Treasury.
American Relief Fund for Lithuanian War Sufferers.
Liberation Fund of Lithuania.
Lithuanian Soldiers Aid Association.
Lithuanian Relief Fund for War Orphans and Widows.
Lithuanian Central War Relief Committee.

APPENDIX

Lithuanian American Relief Committee.
Lithuanian Catholic Truth Society.
Lithuanian Priests Association.
Lithuanian Educational Society Motinele.

BOOKS AND PAMPHLETS PUBLISHED IN BEHALF OF INDEPENDENT LITHUANIA

"Lithuanica." Published under the auspices of American Relief Fund for Lithuanian War Sufferers, Zvaigzde, Philadelphia, Pa., 1916.

"A Memorandum upon the Lithuanian Nation," Paris, 1911.

"A Sketch of the Lithuanian Nation," Paris, 1912.

"The Lithuanian, Ruthenian, Jewish and Polish Questions," London, 1915.

"Lithuania and the Autonomy of Poland," London, 1915.

"The Lithuanian Review," Philadelphia, Pa.

"Pro-Lithuania," Lausanne, Switzerland.

"The Misery of the Lithuanian Refugees in Russia," Lausanne, Switzerland, 1915.

"Sidelights on Life in Lithuania," Washington, D. C.

"Free Lithuania." A collection of articles on Lithuania and Lithuanians, A. Milukas & Co., Philadelphia, Pa., 1917.

"Lithuania in Retrospect and Prospect," by John Szlupas, M.D., New York, Lithuanian Press Association of America, 1915.

"Essay on the Past, Present and Future of Lithuania," by John Szlupas, Stockholm.

"The Lithuanians." Address of Charles L. Brown, President Judge, Municipal Court, Philadelphia, Pa., January 4, 1917.

"Lithuania: Facts Supporting Her Claim for Re-establishment as Independent Nation," Dr. J. J. Bielskis, Washington, D. C.

"Case of Lithuania for Independence," Washington, D. C., 1918. (Also Congressional Record, S. Doc. 305.)

French

"Mémoire sur la Nation Lituanienne."

"La Nation Lituanienne," Paris.

"Lituaniens et Polonais," par A. Jakstis, Paris, 1913.

"L'Eglise Polonaise en Lituanie," par Mgr. C. Propolanis, Paris, 1914.

"La Situation de l'Eglise Catholique en Lituanie," par Dr. J. Gabrys, Paris, 1915.

"La Lituanie Religieuse," par A. Viskontas, Ph.D., D.D., Genève, 1917.

"La Lituanie russe au point de vue statistique et ethnographique," par A. Viskontas, Genève, 1917.

APPENDIX 155

"La Lituanie," par A. Vilimavicius, Genève, 1918.

"La Lituanie, le territoire occupé, la population et l'orientation de ses idées," par A. Vilimavicius, Genève, 1918.

"Justice Allemande," par C. Rivas, Geneva-Nancy, 1918.

"Occupation Allemande en Lituanie," par C. Rivas, Geneva, 1918.

"La Lituanie dans le passé et dans le présent," par W. St. Vidunas, Genève, 1918.

"La Lituanie sous la Botte allemande," par M. Ragana, Paris, 1917.

"Ober-Ost, le plan annexionniste allemand en Lituanie," par C. Rivas, Lausanne, Switzerland, 1917.

"Les Souffrances du peuple Lituanien," par P. L. K., Lausanne, Switzerland, 1917.

"Pro Lituania," Lausanne, Switzerland.

"Carte de la Lituanie," Lausanne, Switzerland.

"La Haute Trahison de 44 Polonais," Lausanne.

"Les Lituaniens d'Amérique," Lausanne, 1918.

"L'Etat Lituanien et le Gouvernement de Suvalkai (Suvalki)," Lausanne, 1918.

"Observations du Délégué du Conseil National Lituanien," Lausanne, 1918.

"La Lituanie sous le Joug Allemand 1915-1918. Le plan annexionniste allemand en Lituanie.

C. Rivas, Librairie Centrale des Nationalités," Lausanne, 1918.

"Le Principaux Artisans de la Renaissance Nationale Lituanienne, Hommes et Choses de Lituanie, avec préface de Mr. Charles Rivet," Lausanne, 1918.

LITHUANIAN CATHOLIC TRUTH SOCIETY
REV. F. JAKSZTYS, *President*,
29 Davis St., Harrison, N. J.
REV. A. KODIS, *Treasurer*,
207 York St., Brooklyn, N. Y.
REV. A. M. MILUKAS, *Secretary*,
94 Hull Ave., Maspeth, L. I.

UNIVERSITY OF CALIFORNIA LIBRARY
Los Angeles

This book is DUE on the last date stamped below.